Magical Unicorn

Coloring Book for Girls
Aged 4 to 10 Years

This Book Belongs To

____

____

____

____

Copyright © 2024 by Al&Vy

Magical Unicorn
Coloring Book

✓ **40 Adorable coloring pages** 🖼

✓ **Great for young, aspiring artists** 🎨

✓ **Ideal for crayons, markers, or colored pencils** ✏

✓ **Large print page format: 8.5 x 11 inches** 📖

✓ **Single-sided pages to avoid bleed-through, ensuring your masterpieces remain pristine** 🎨

✓ **Activity to help the child relax and explore creativity** ♥

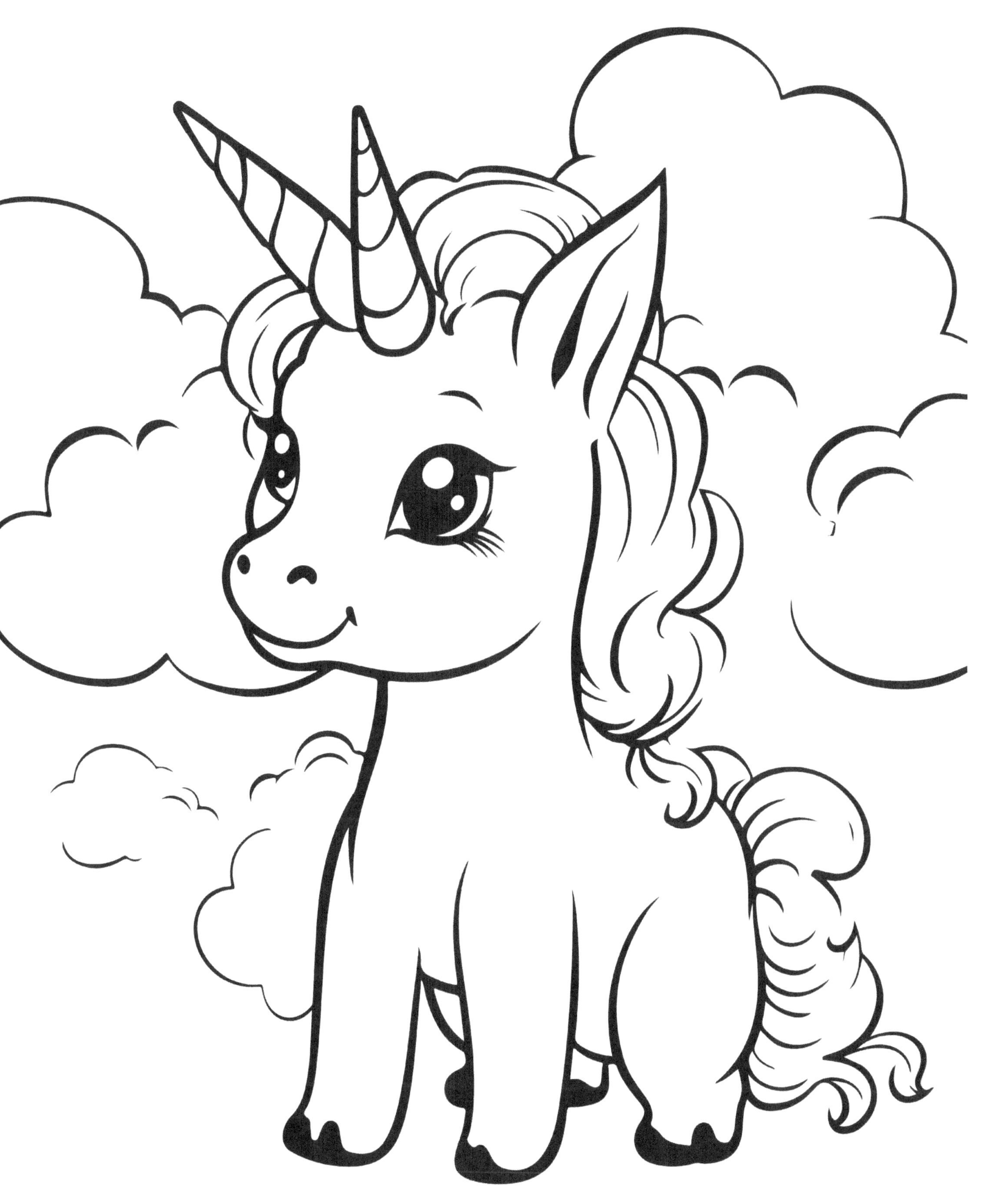

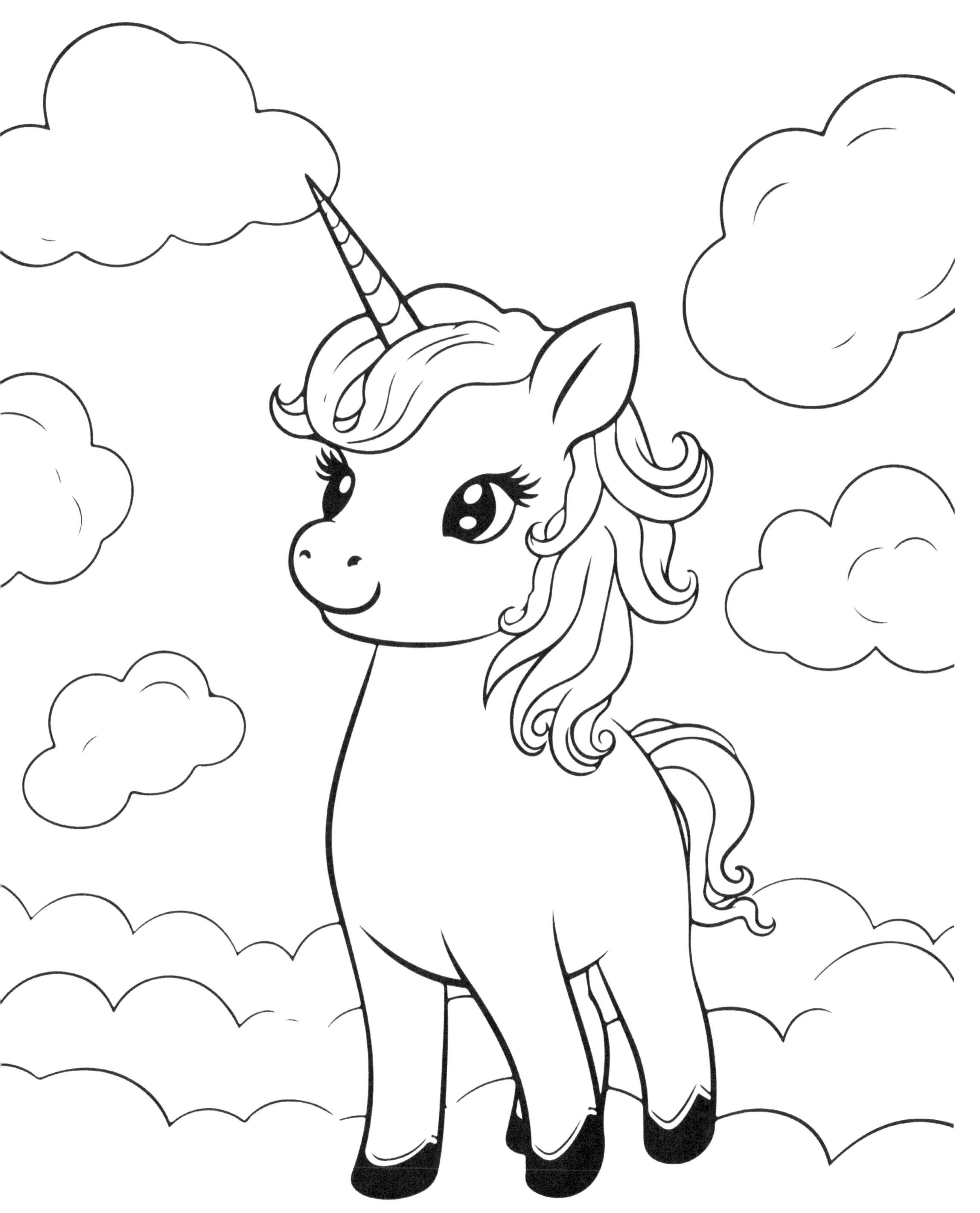

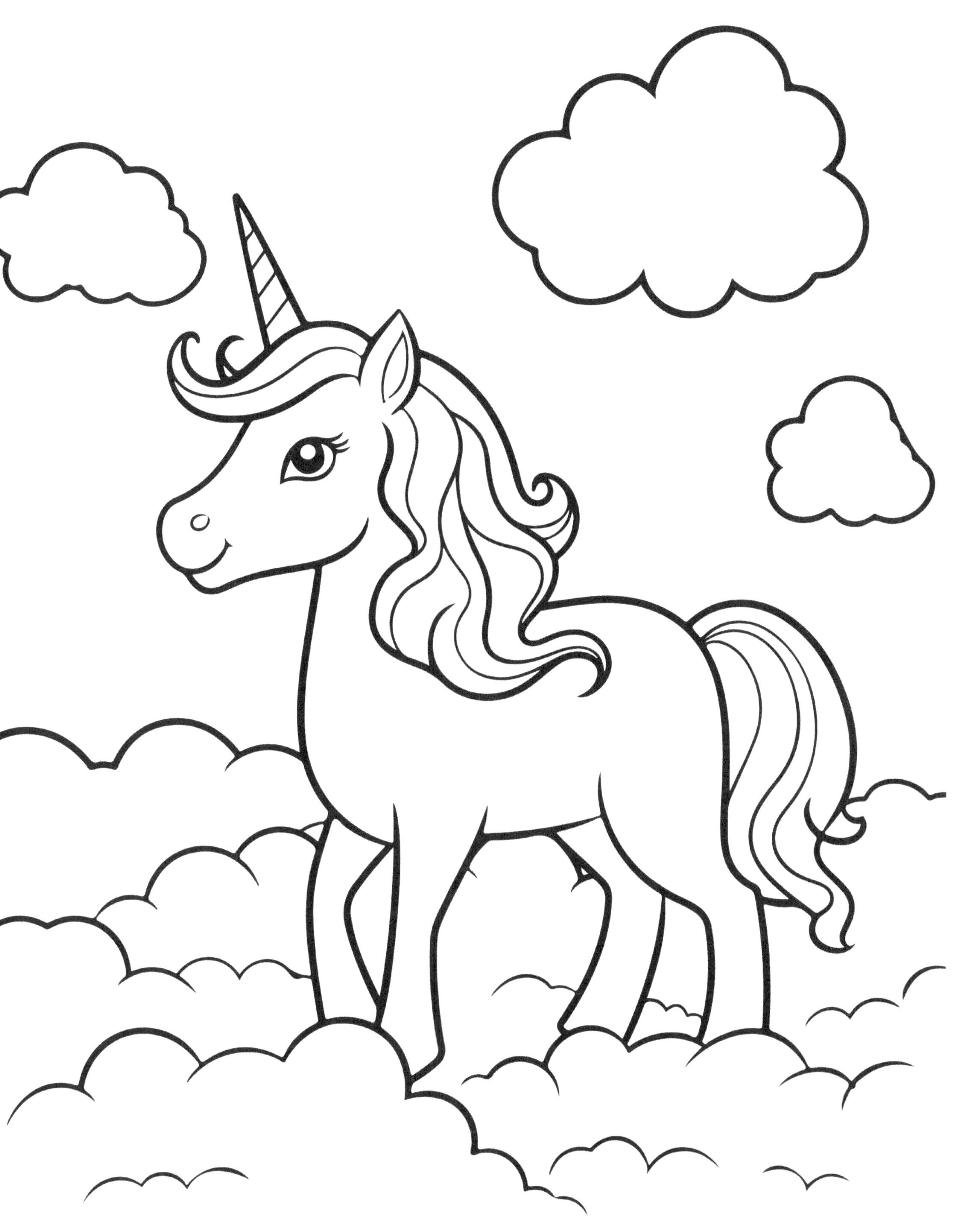

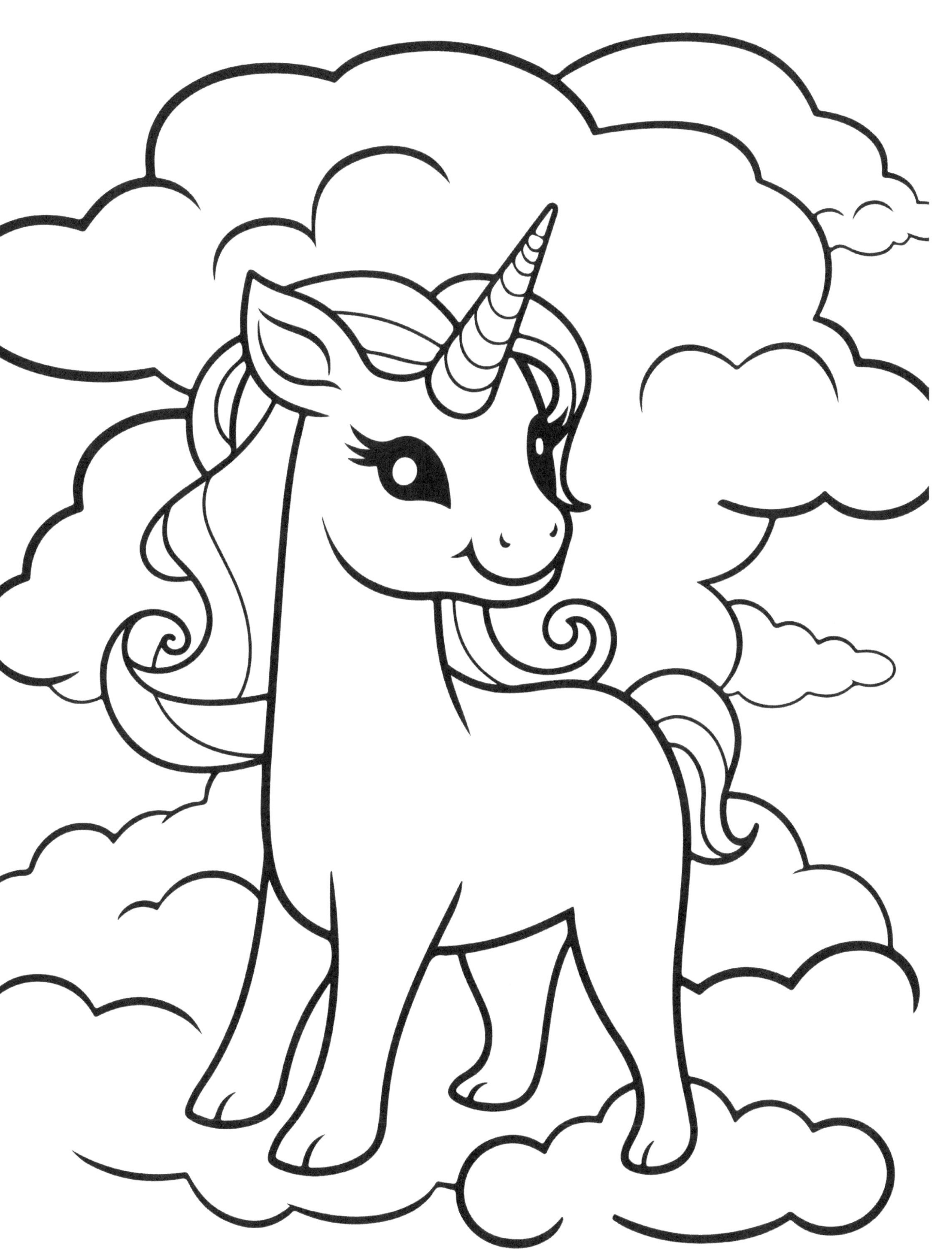

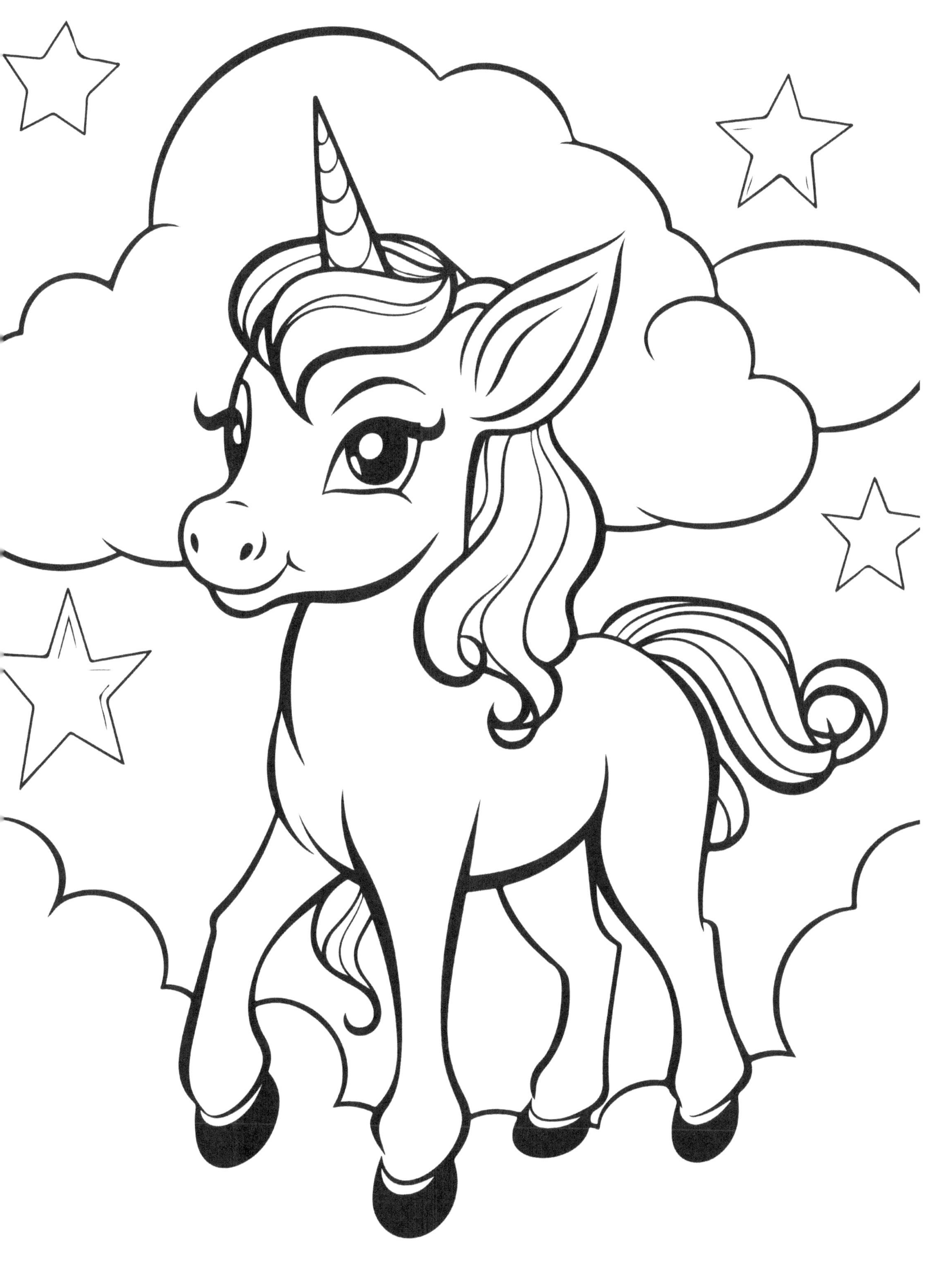

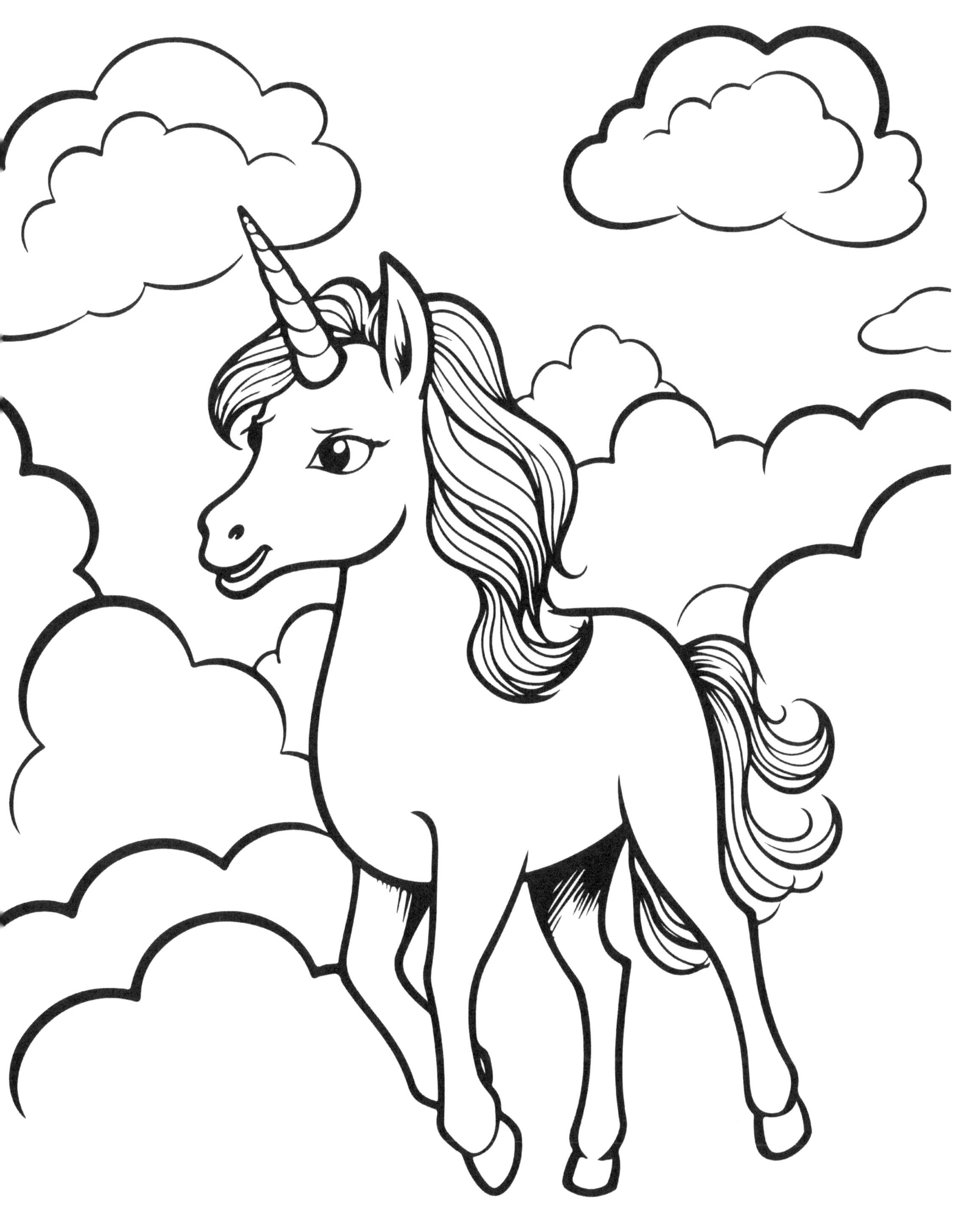

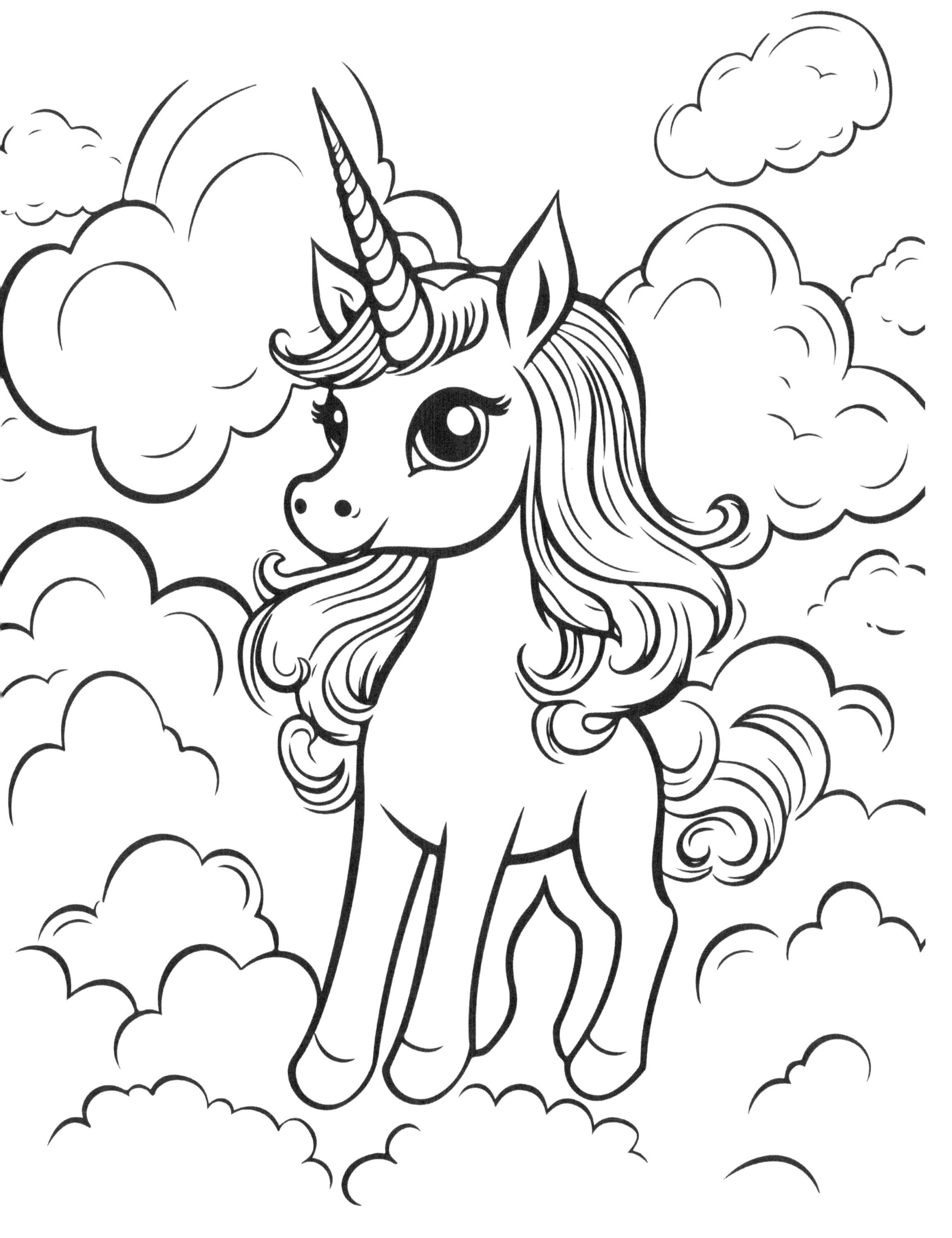

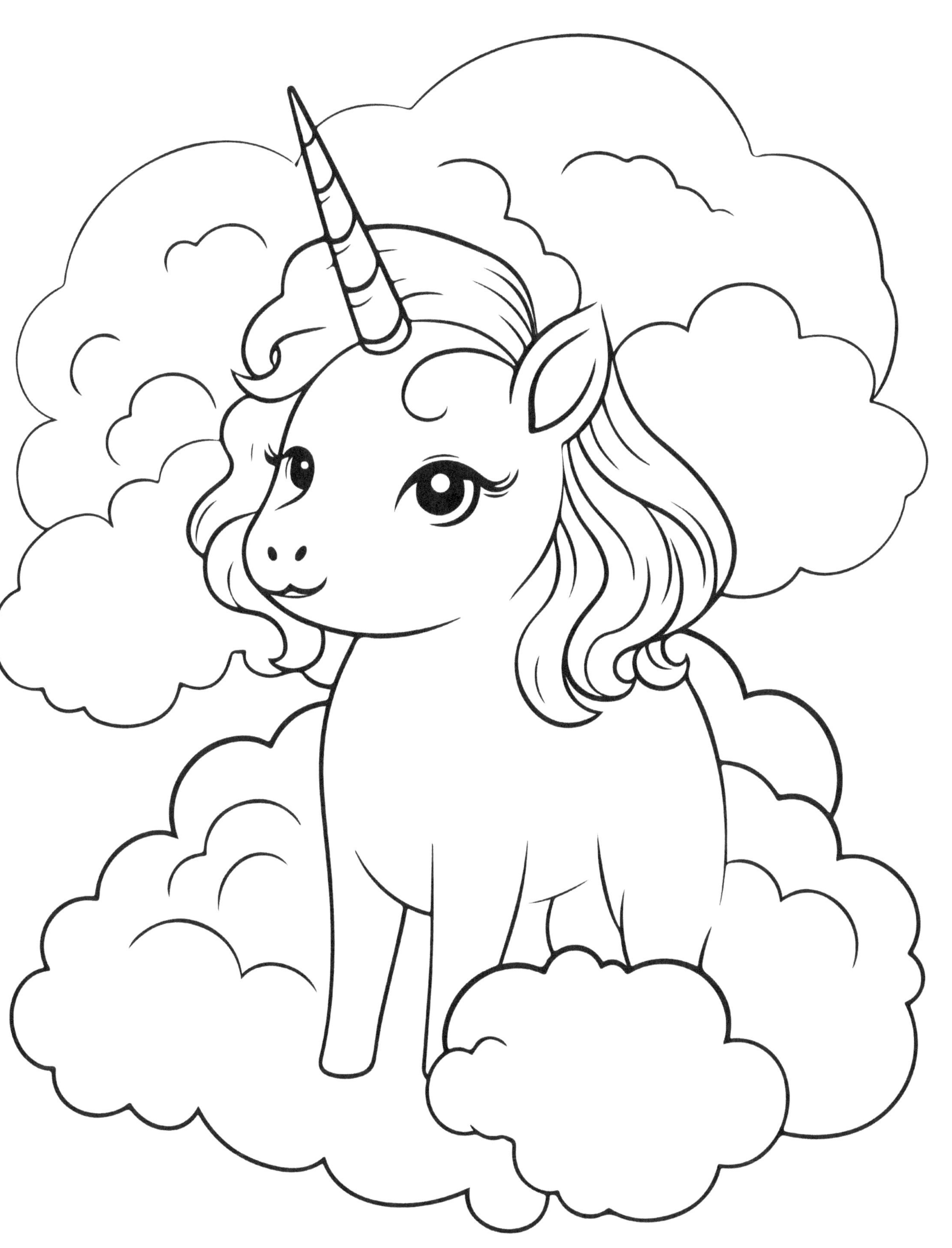

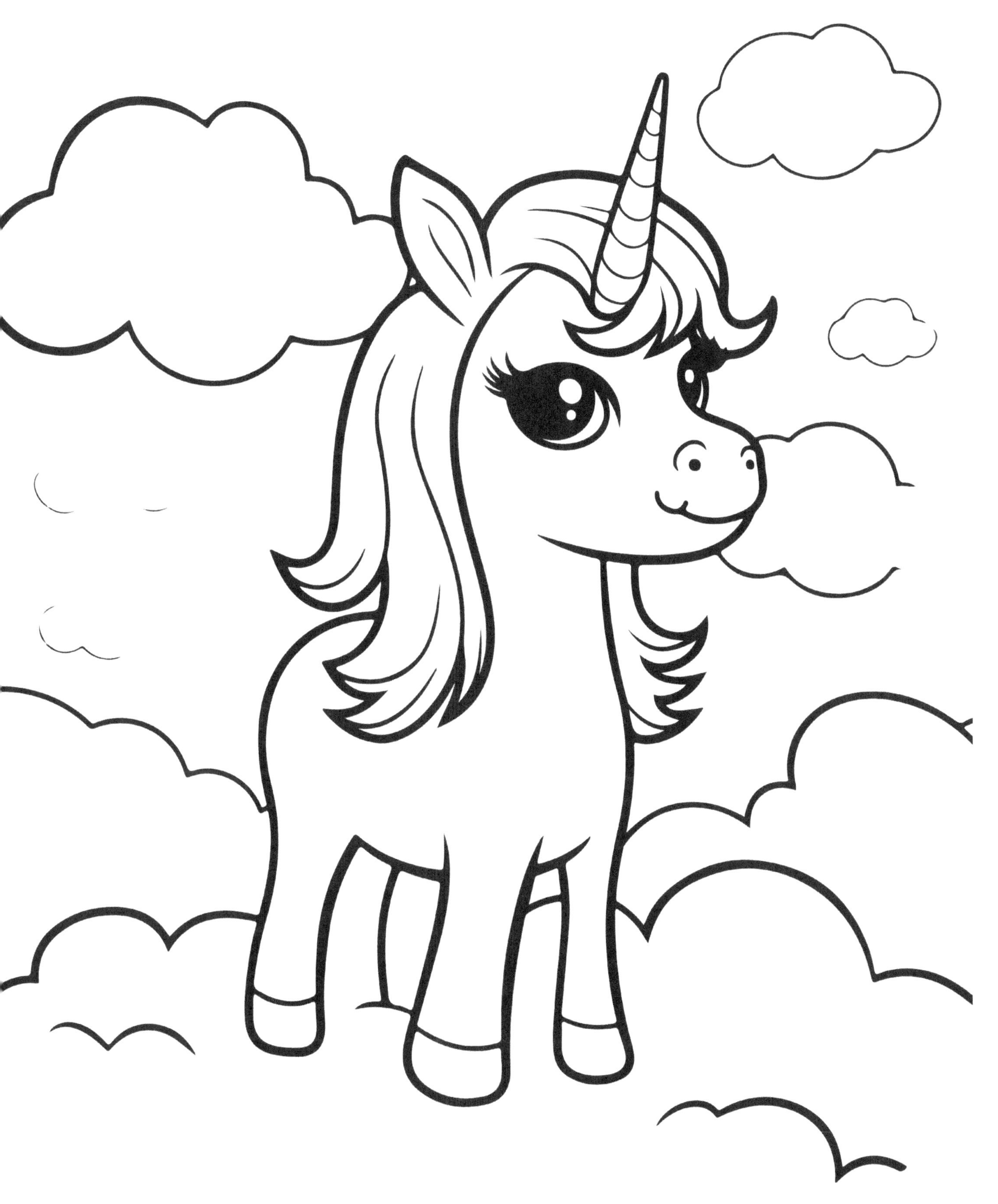

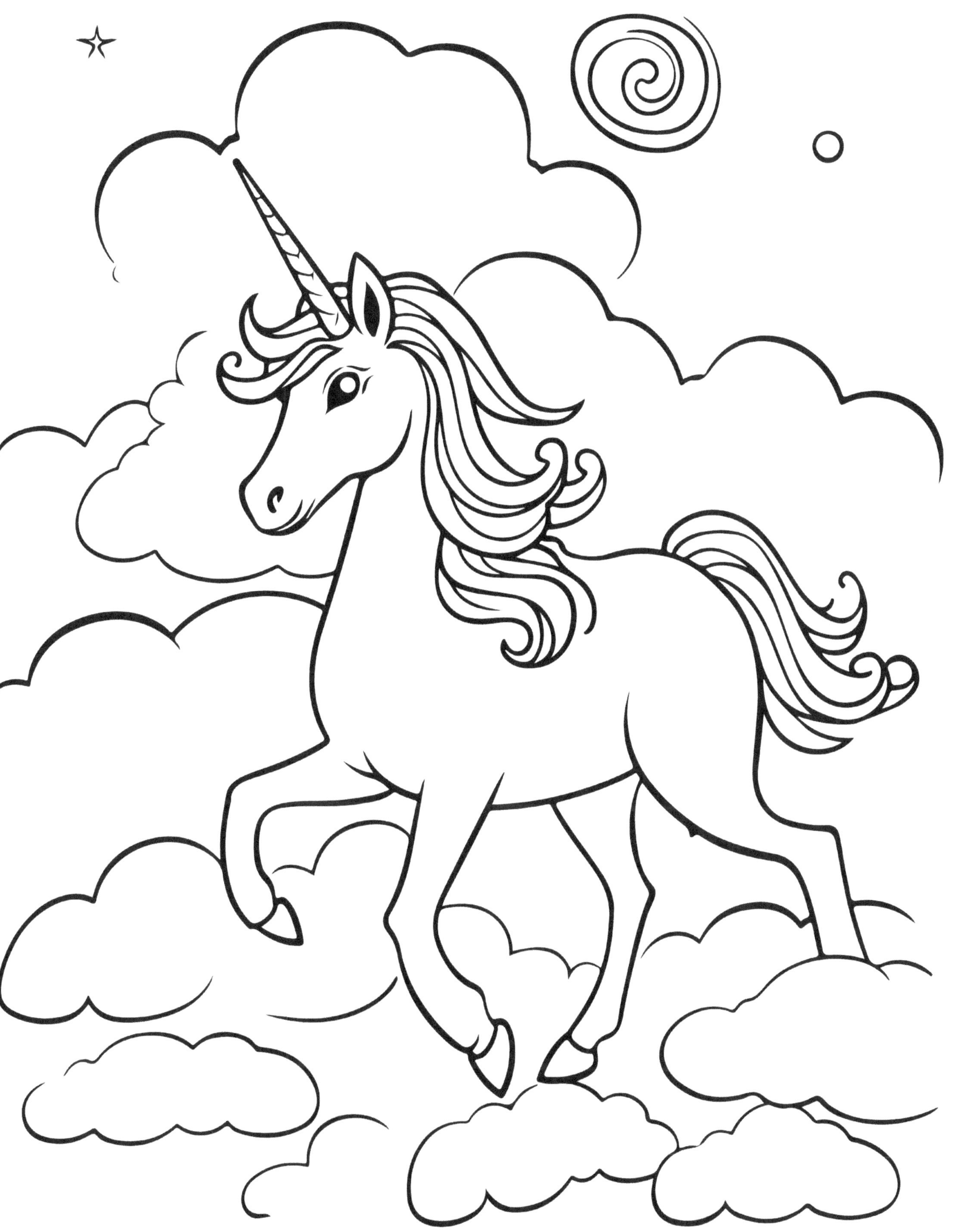

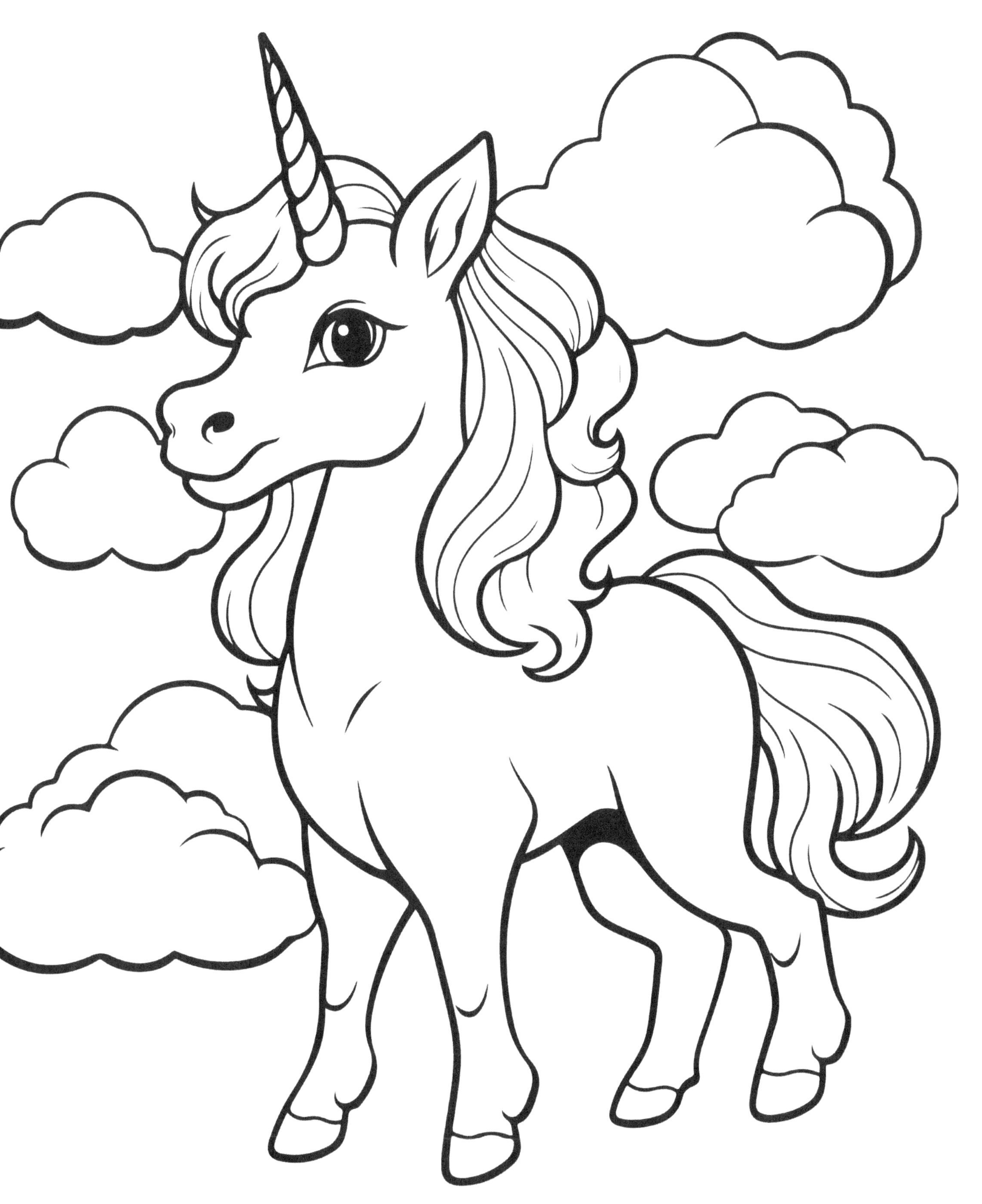

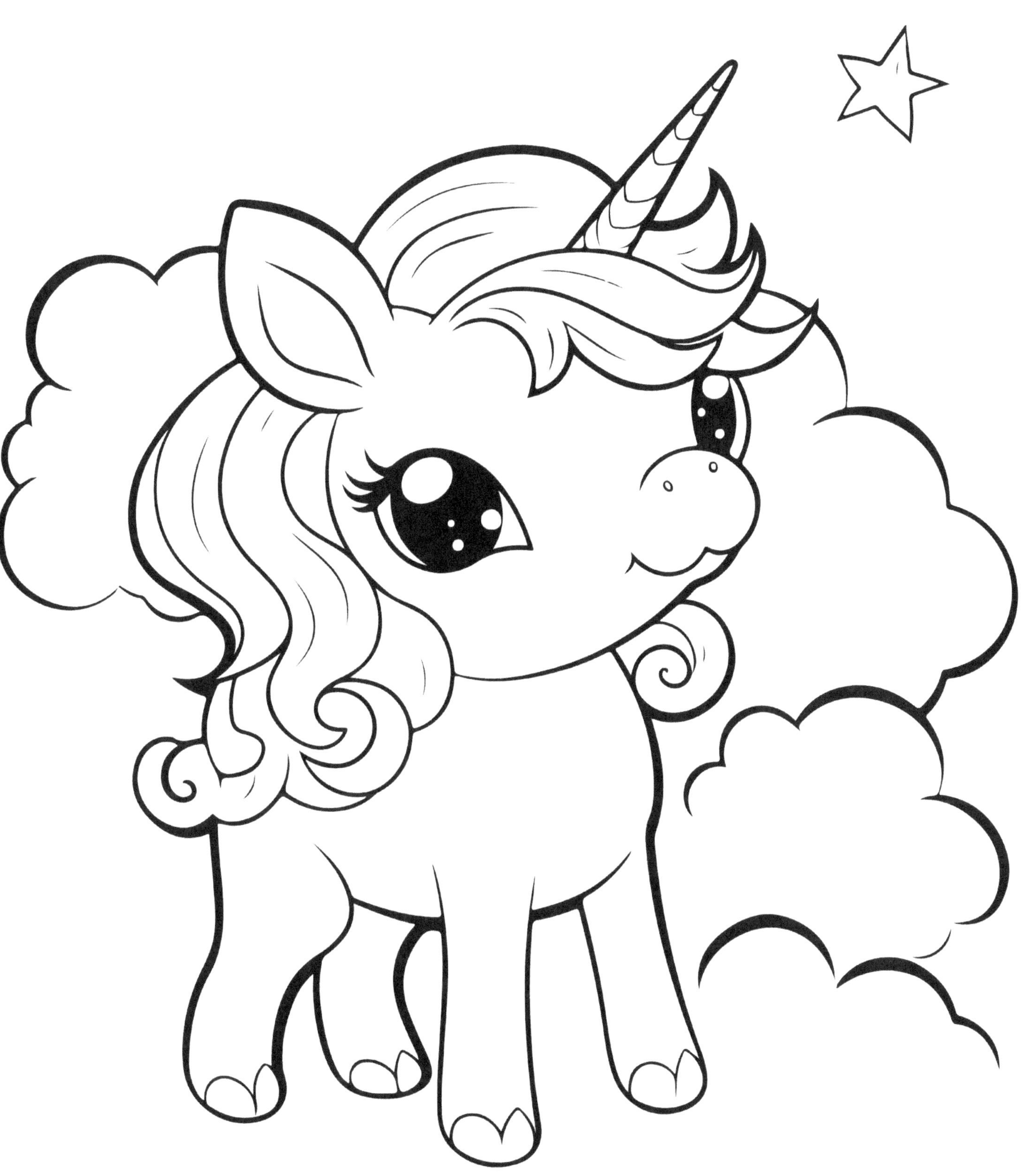

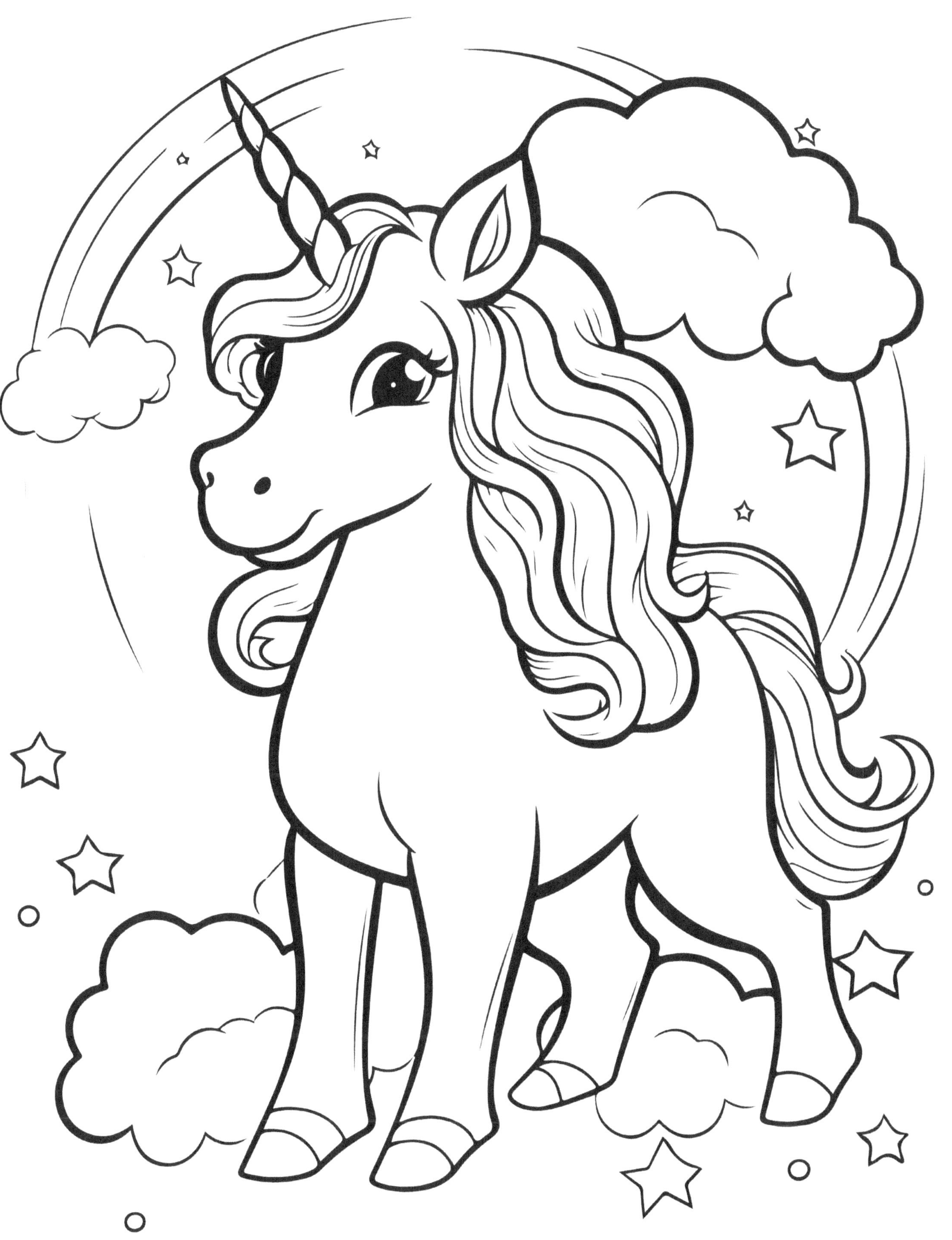

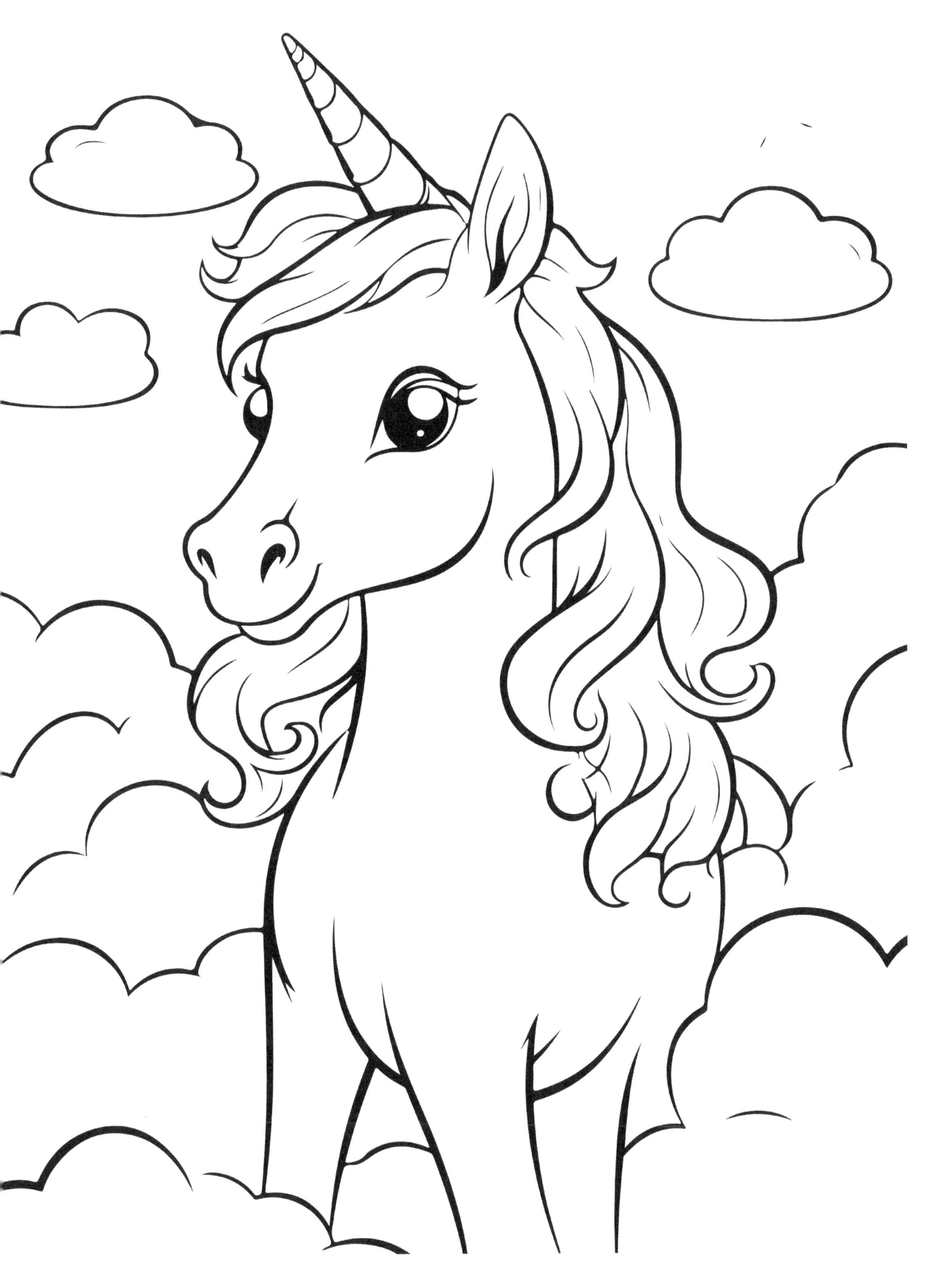

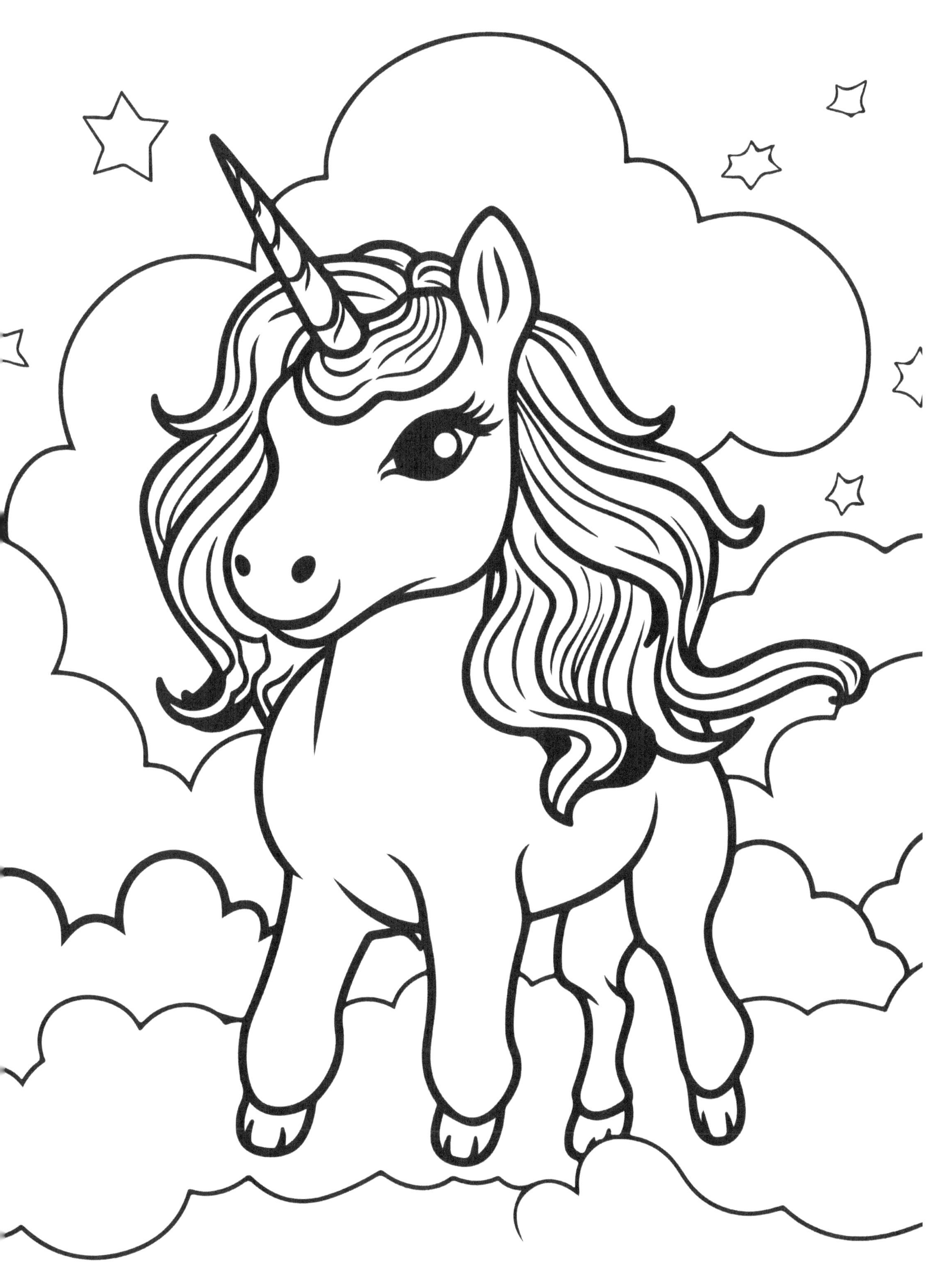

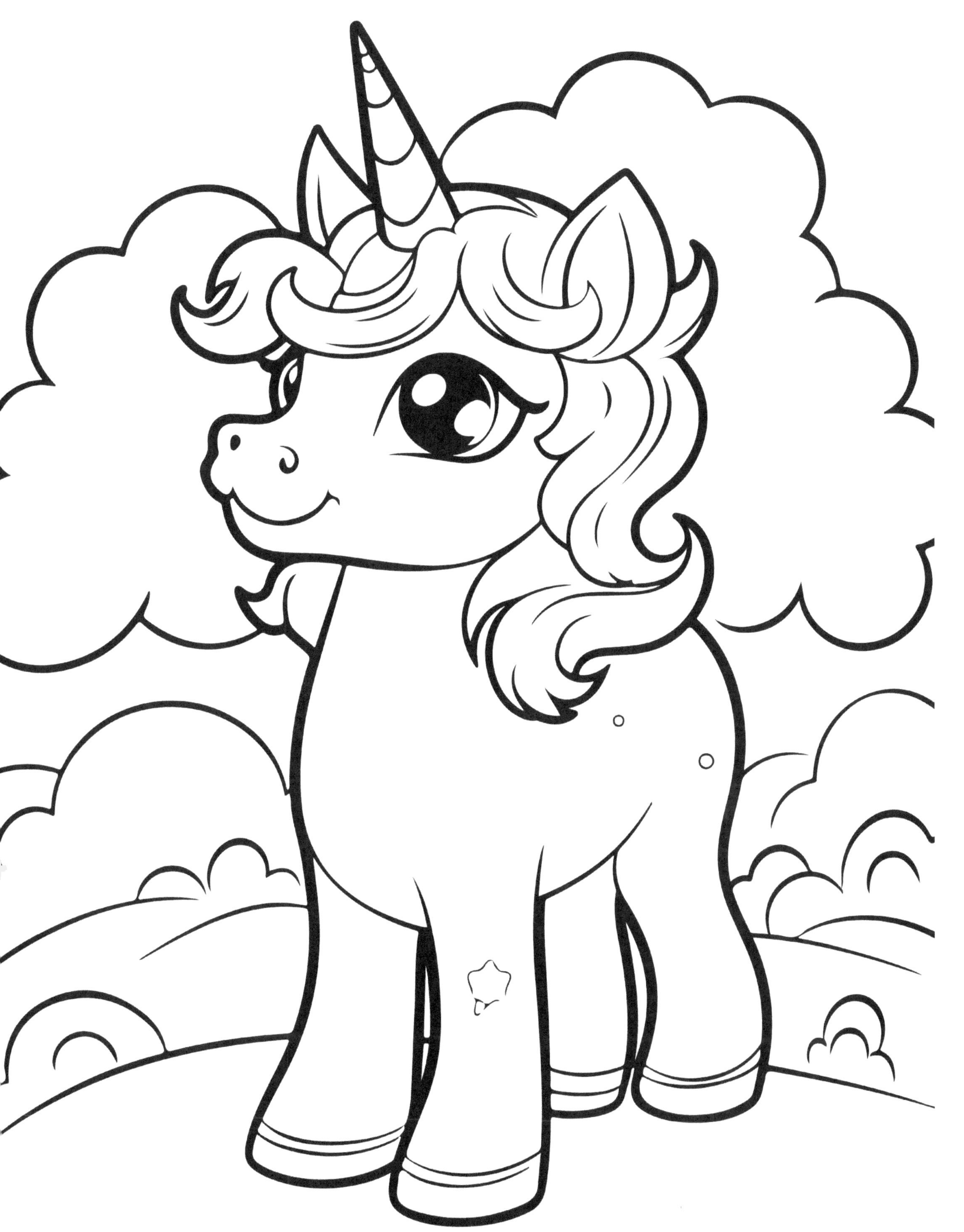

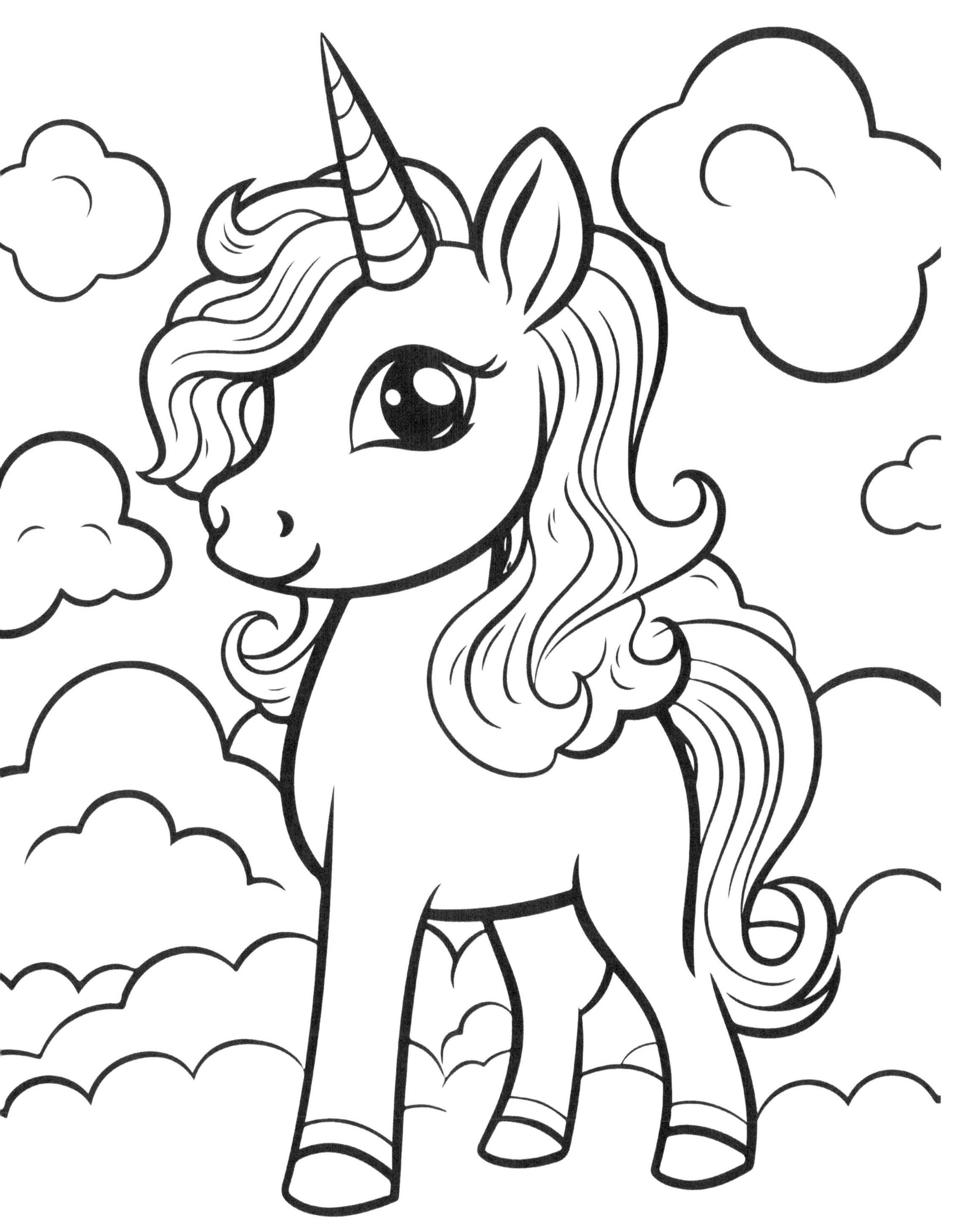

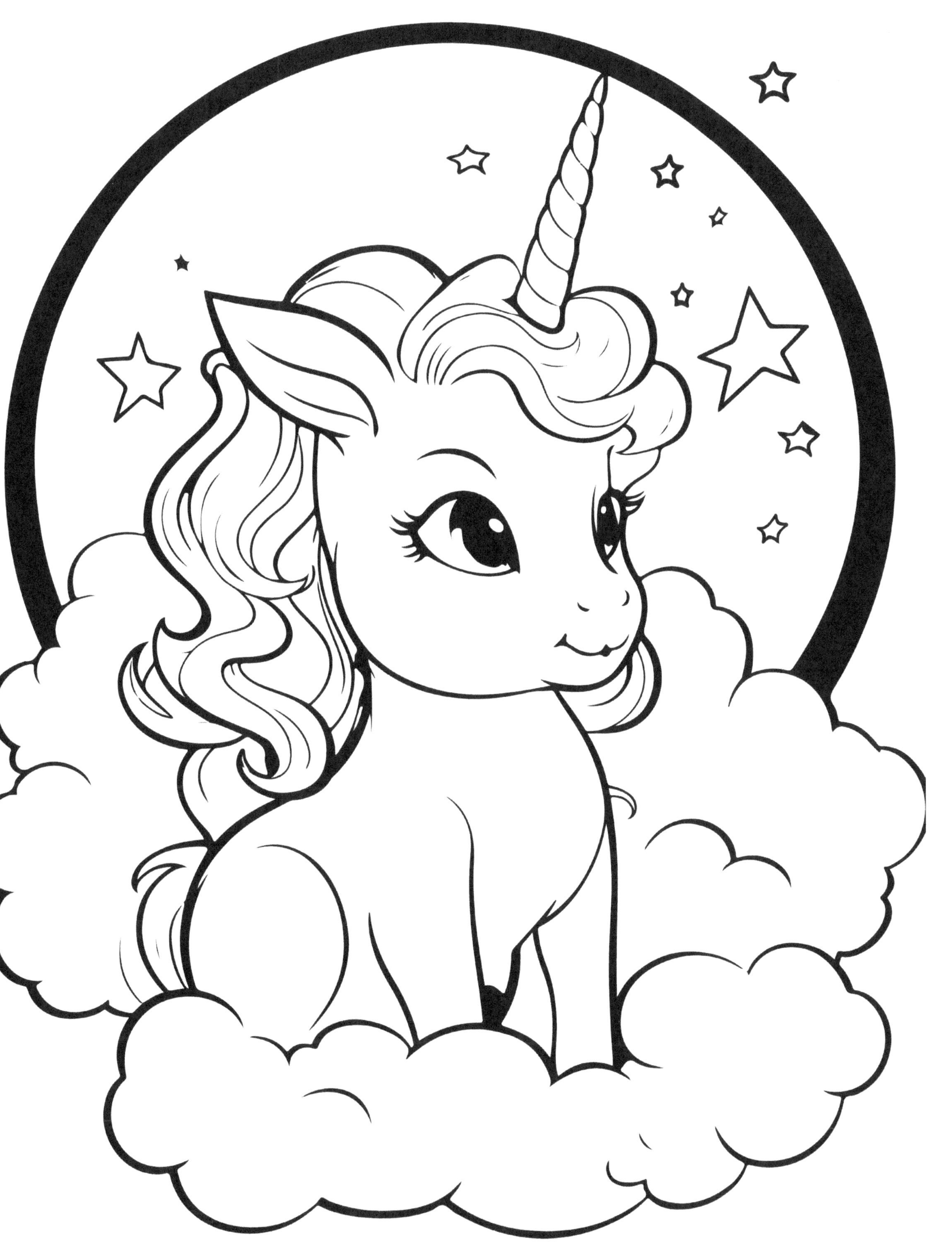

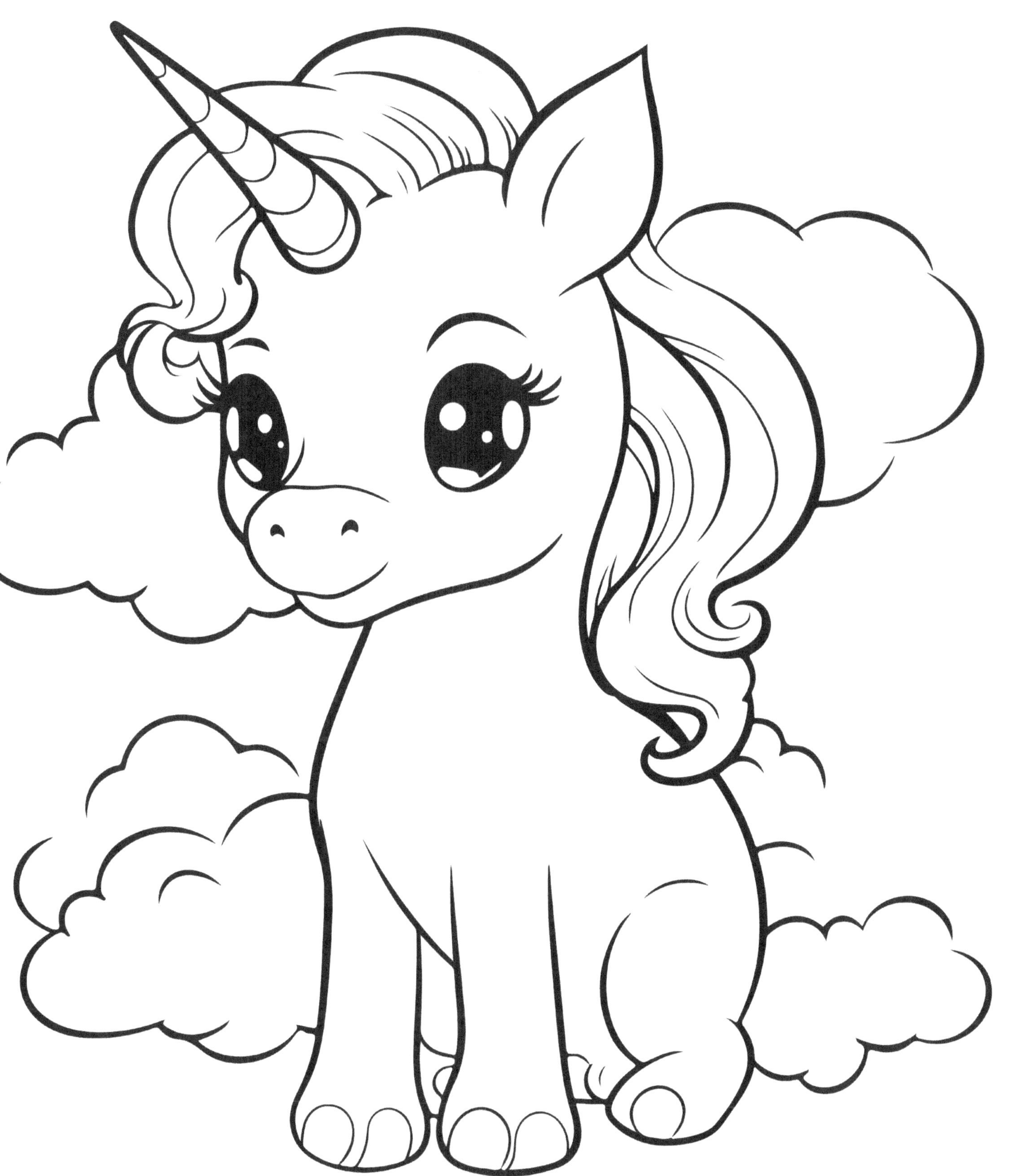

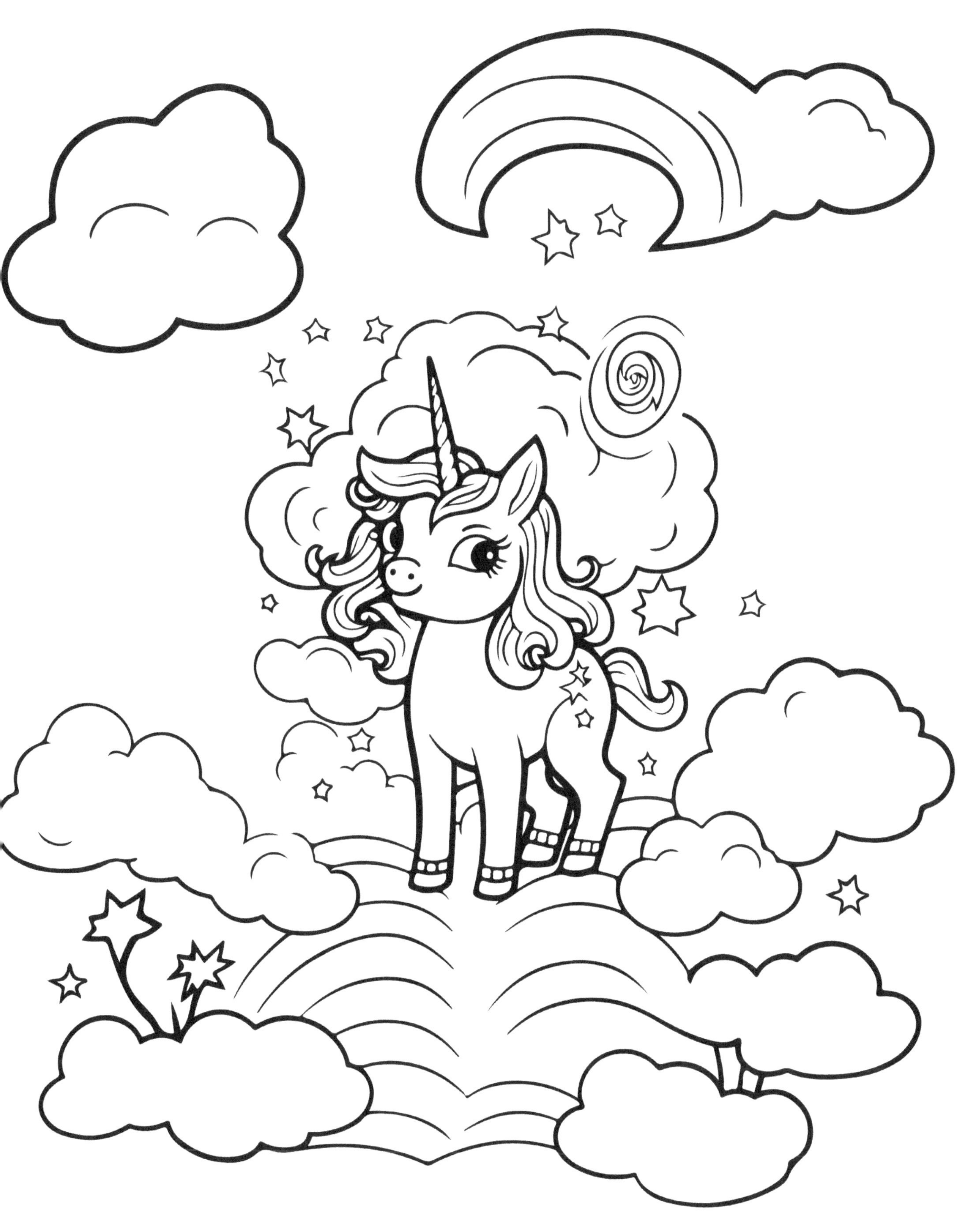

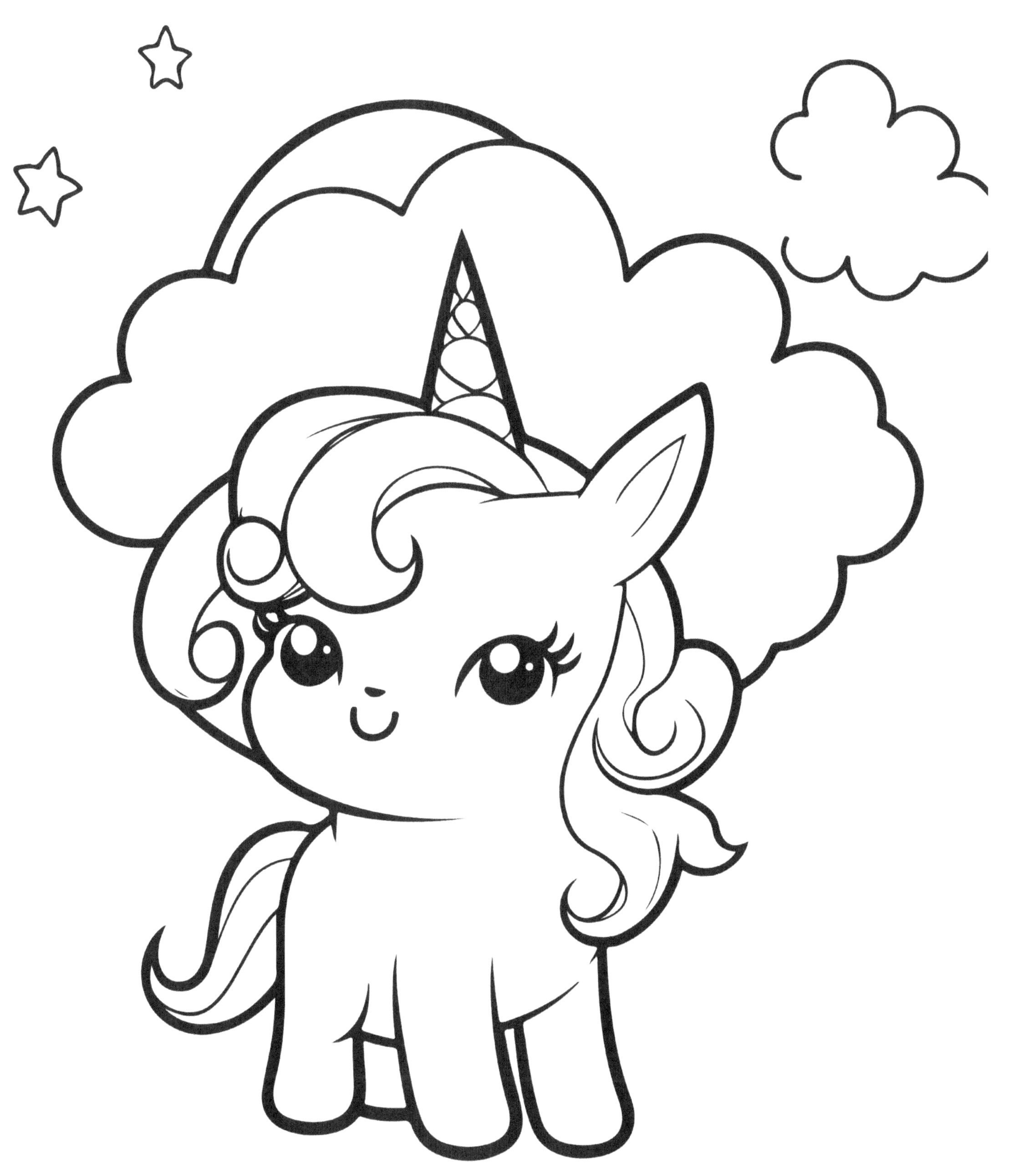

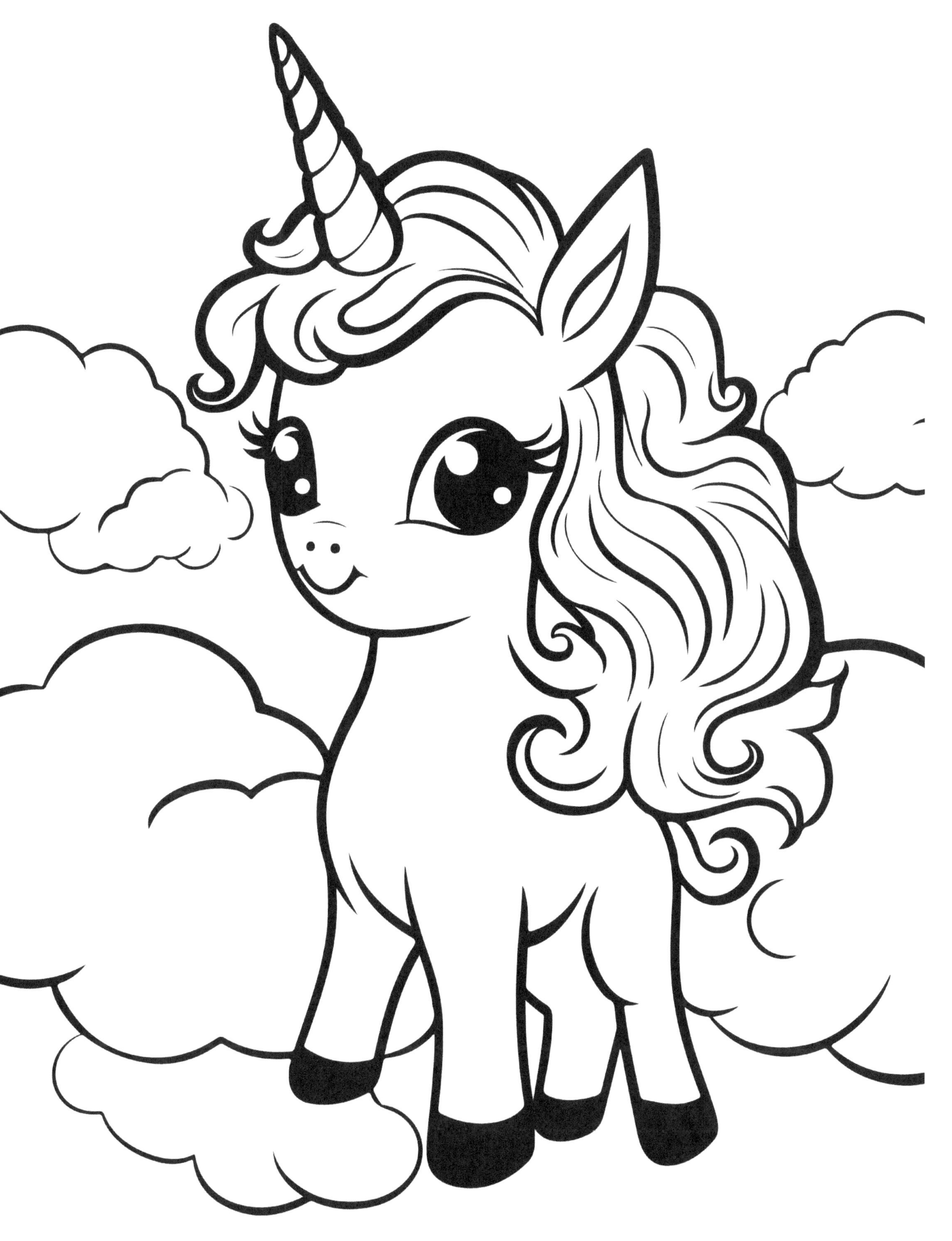

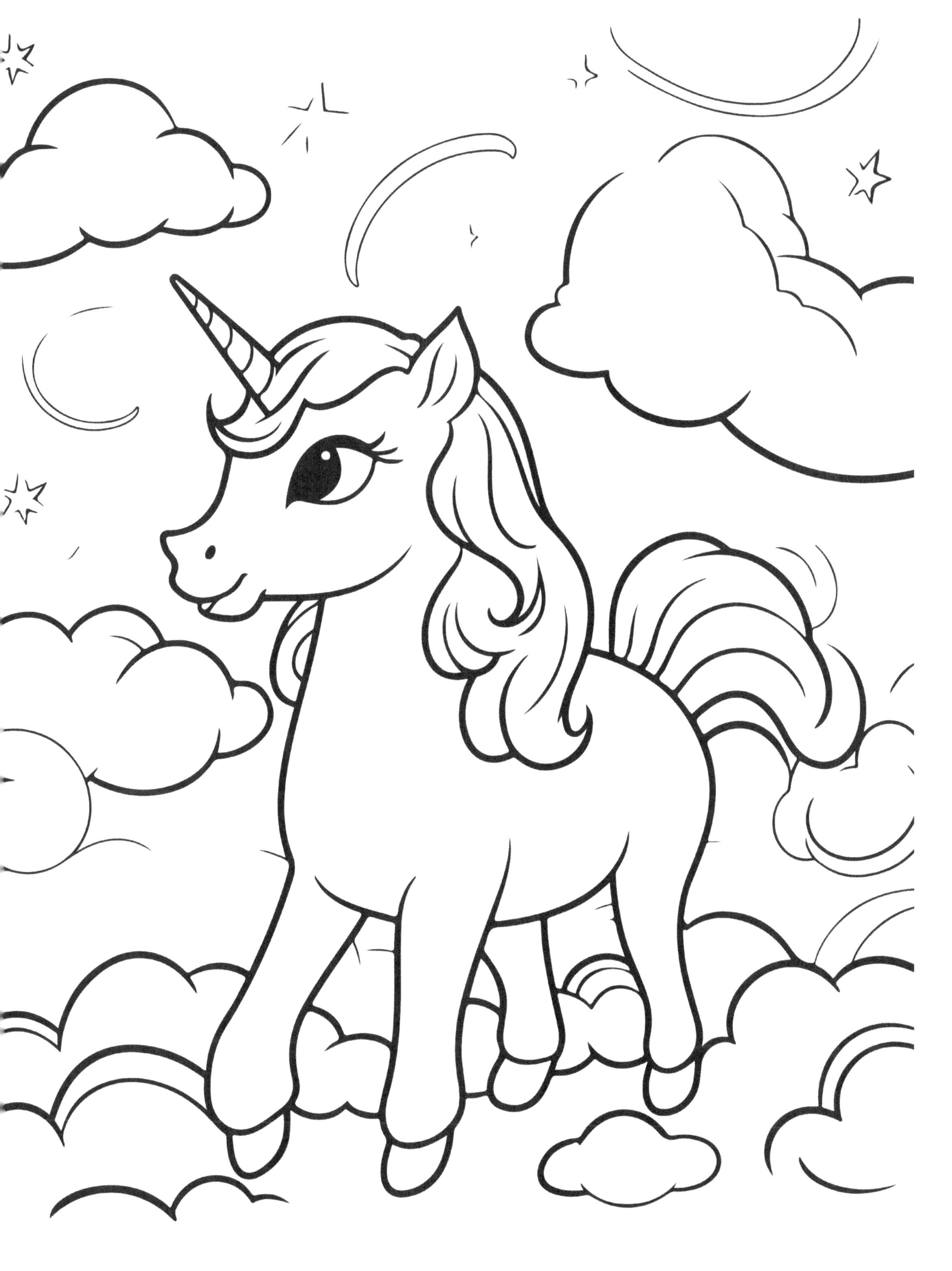

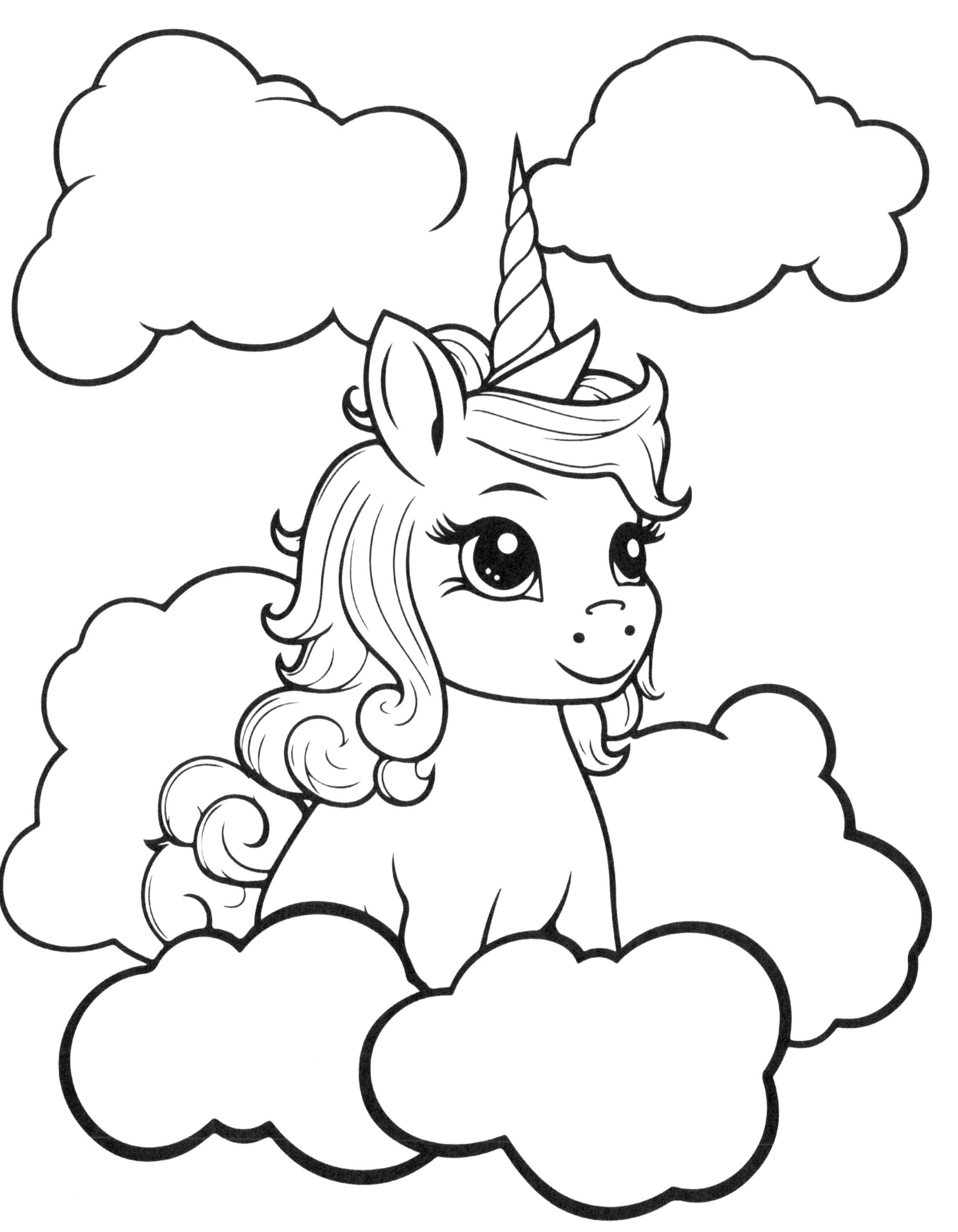

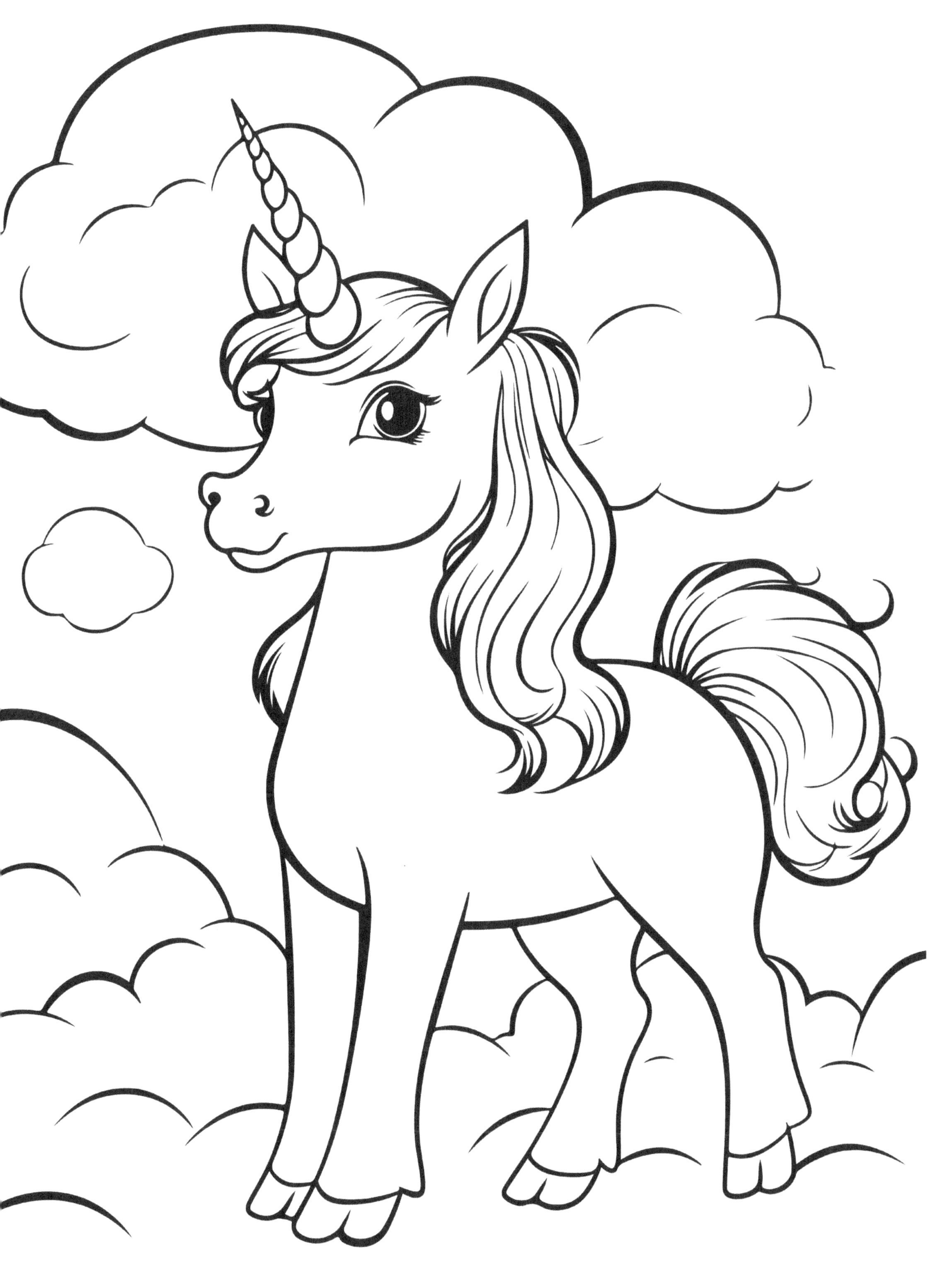

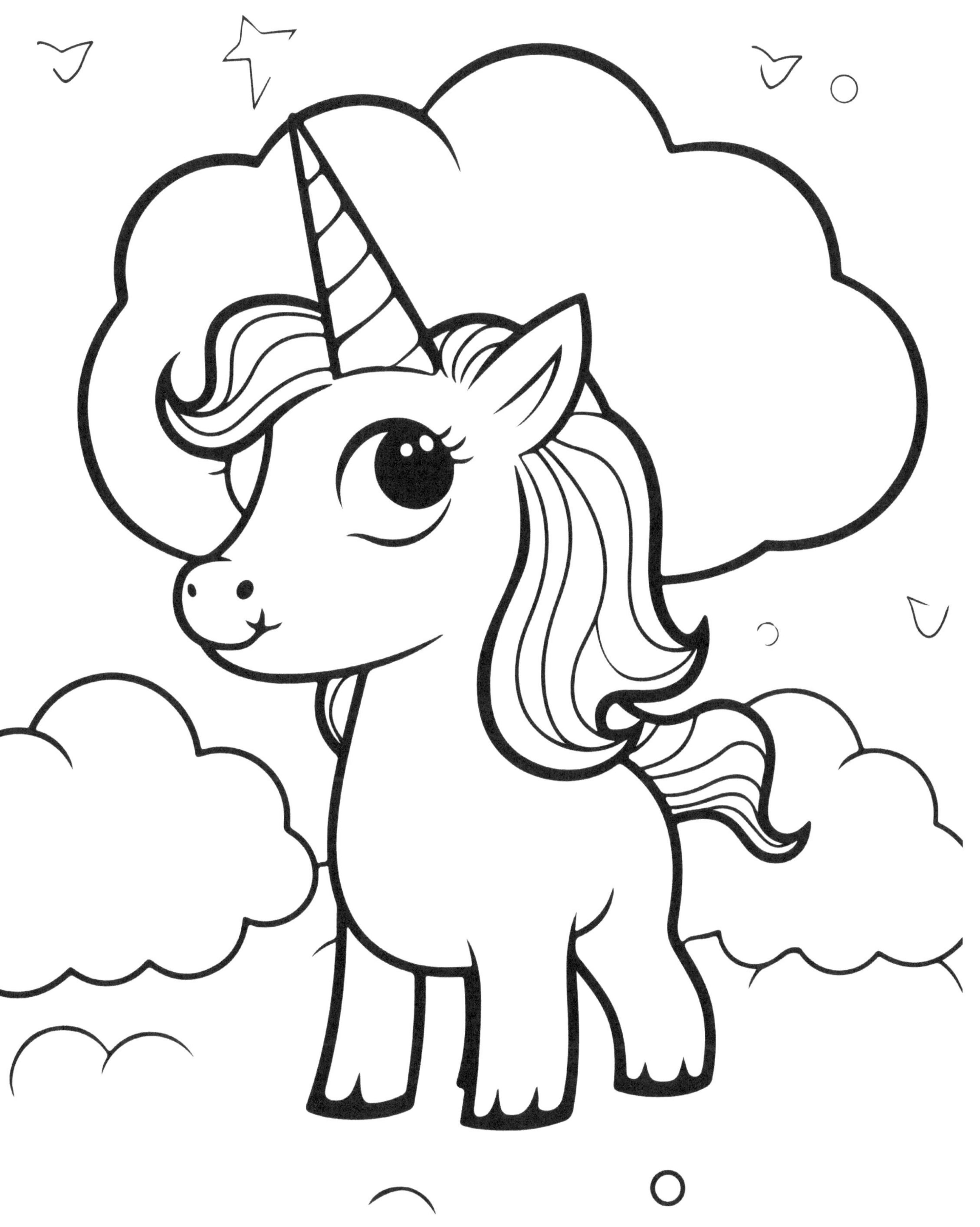

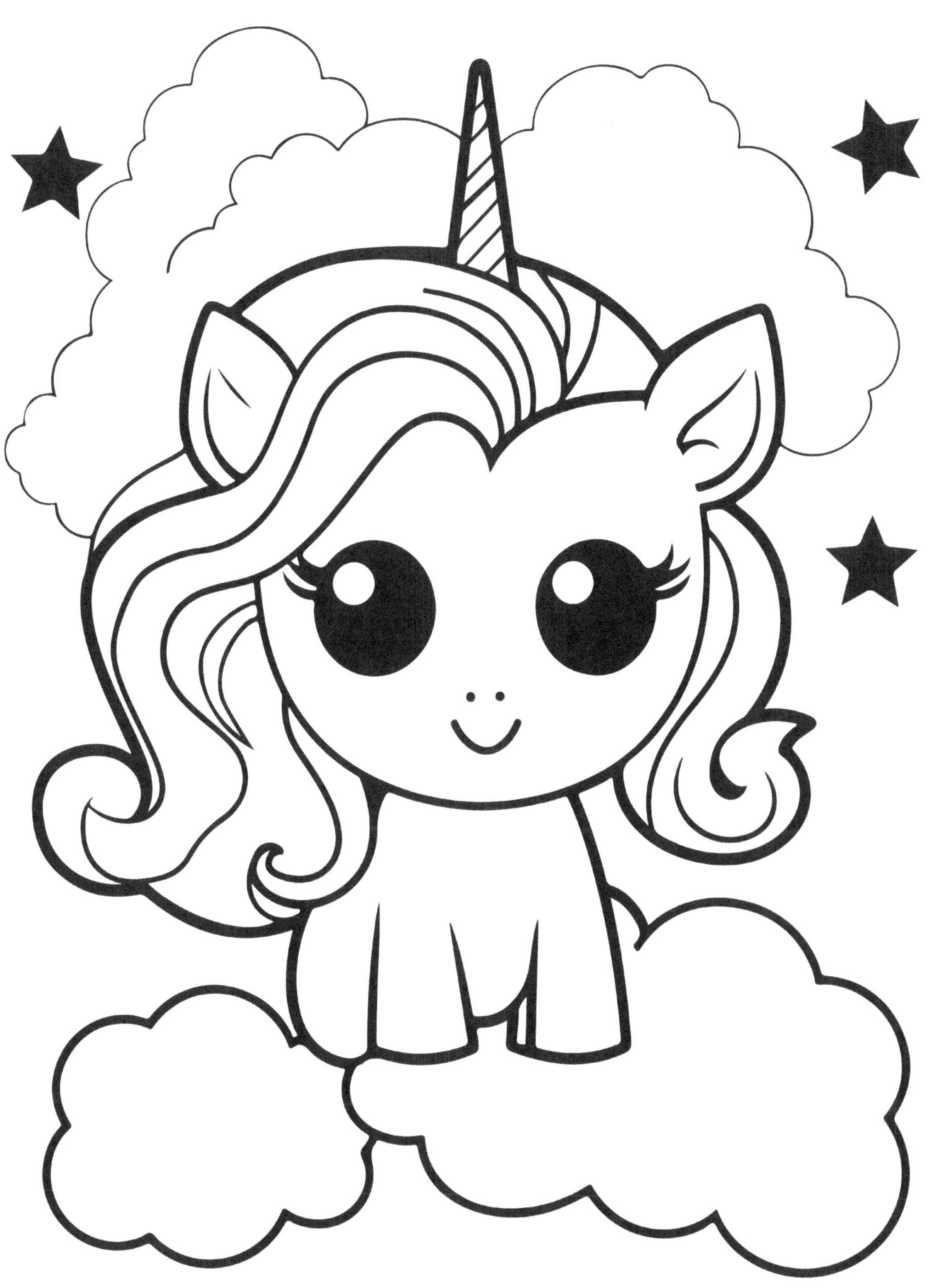

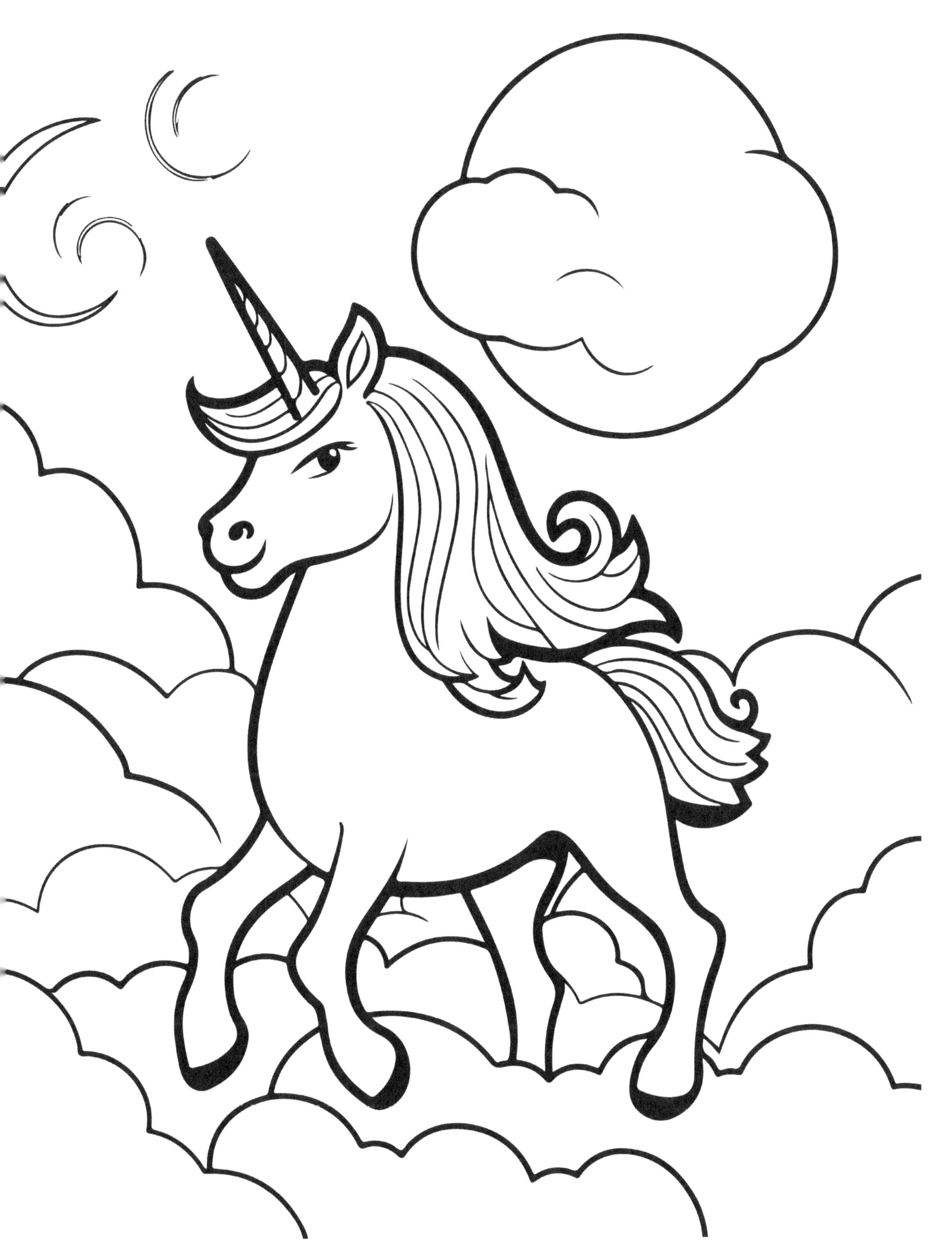

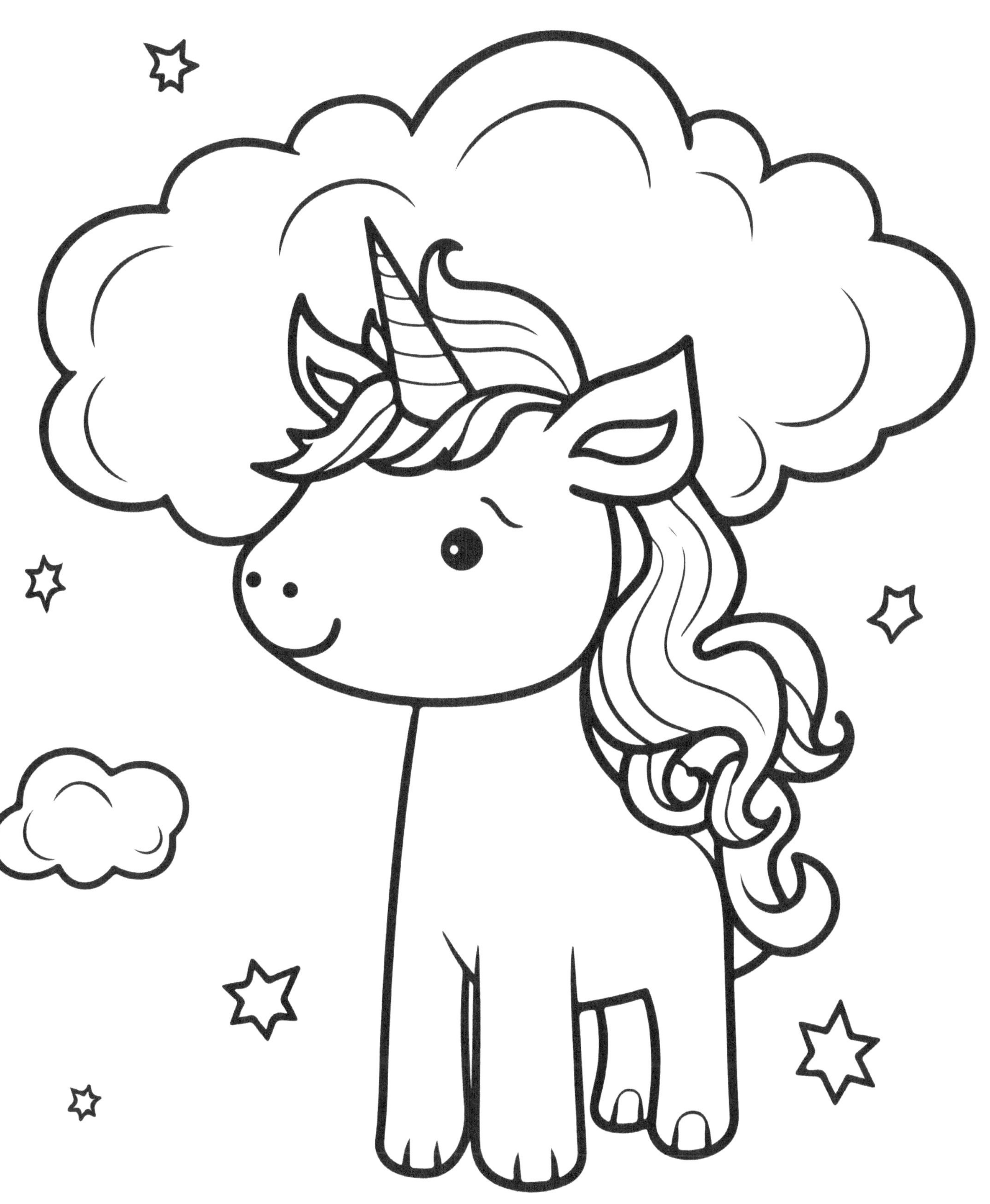

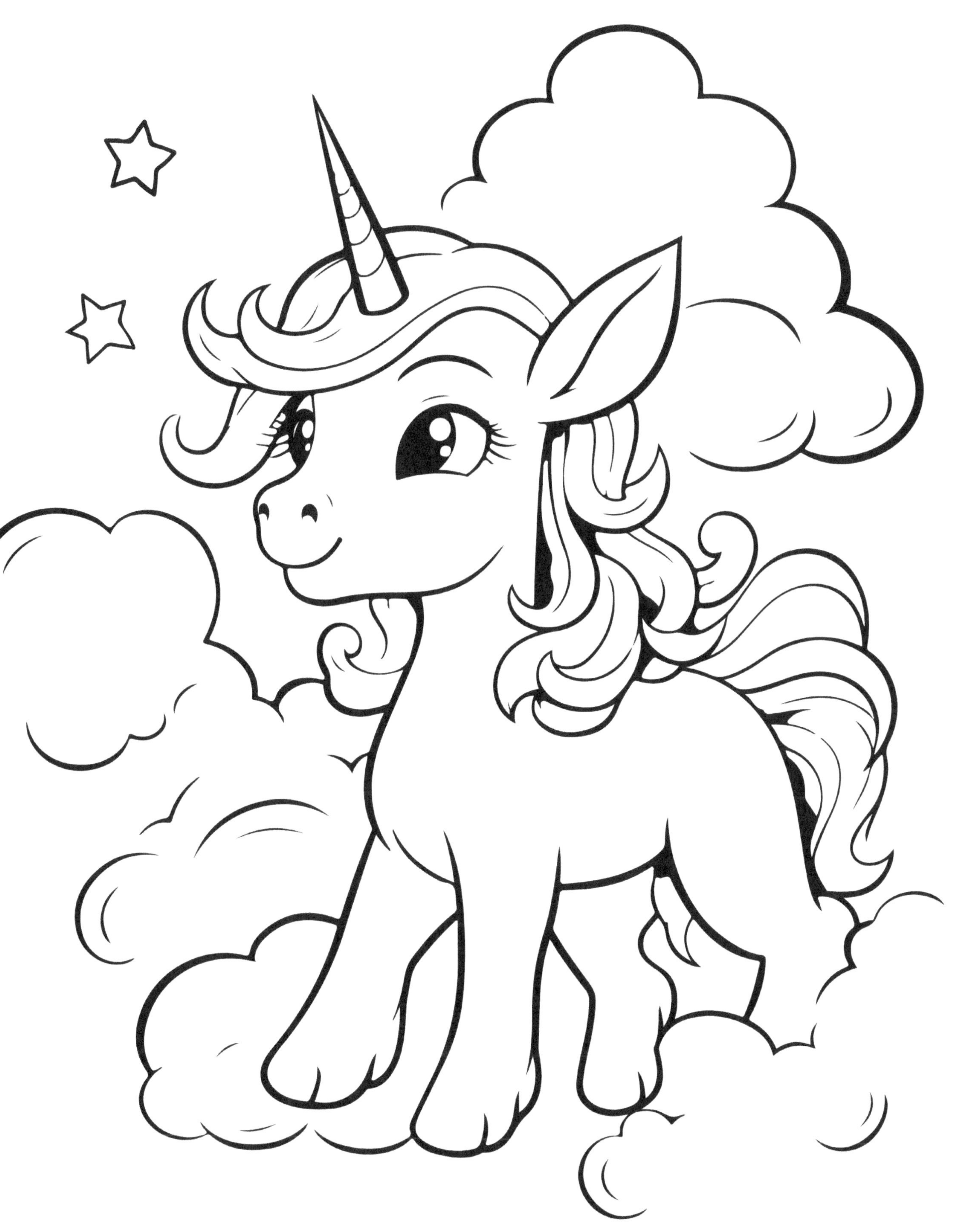

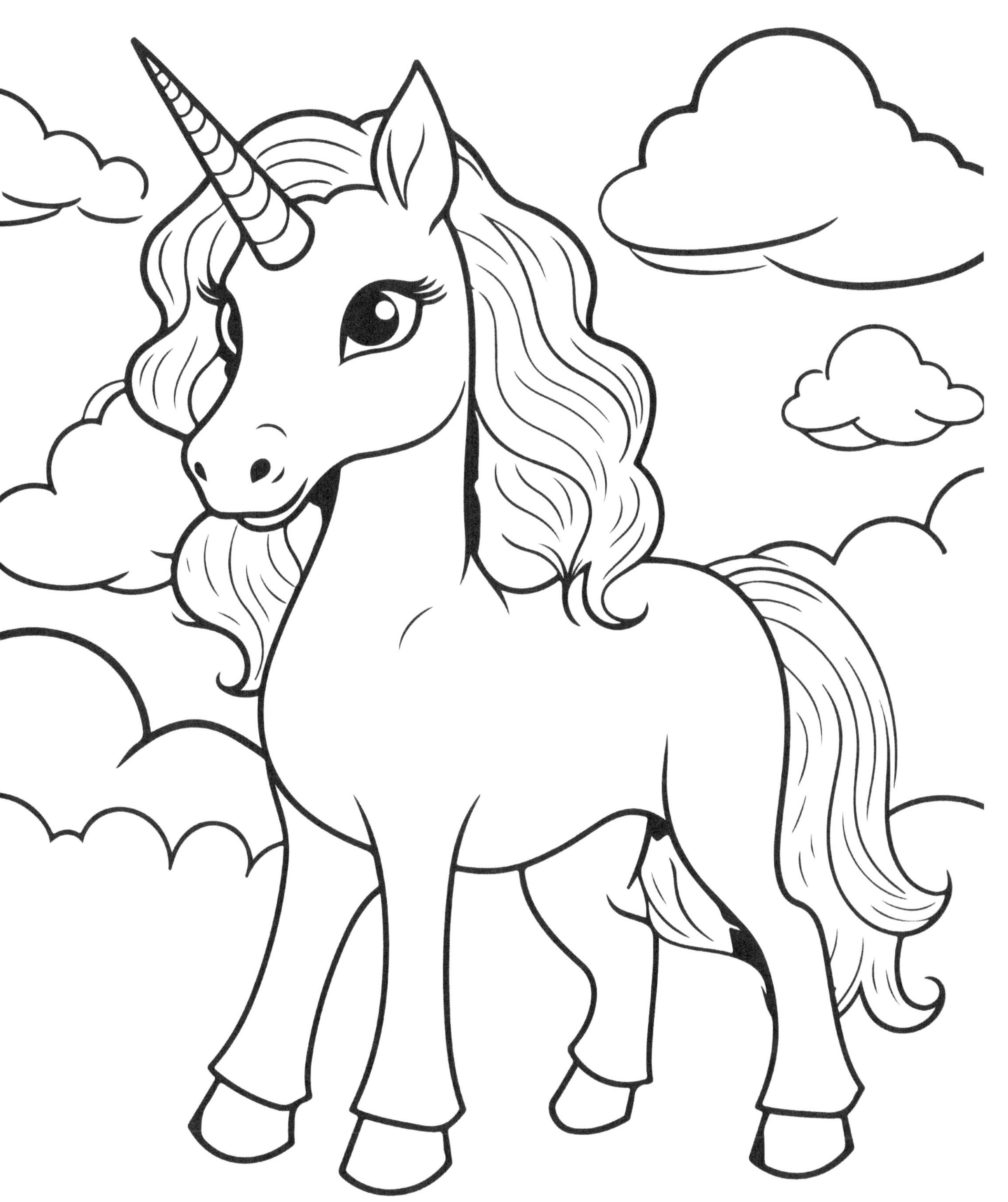

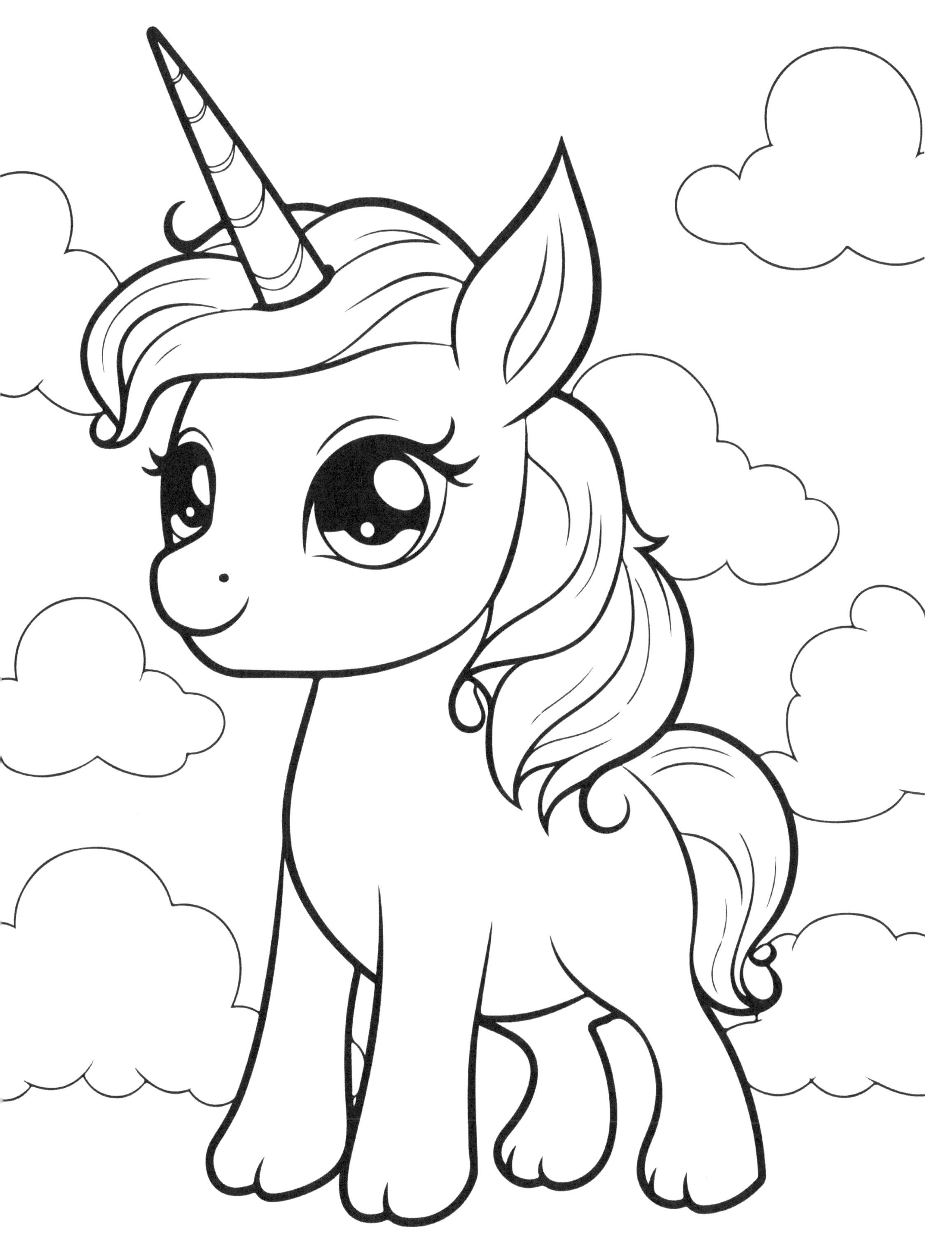

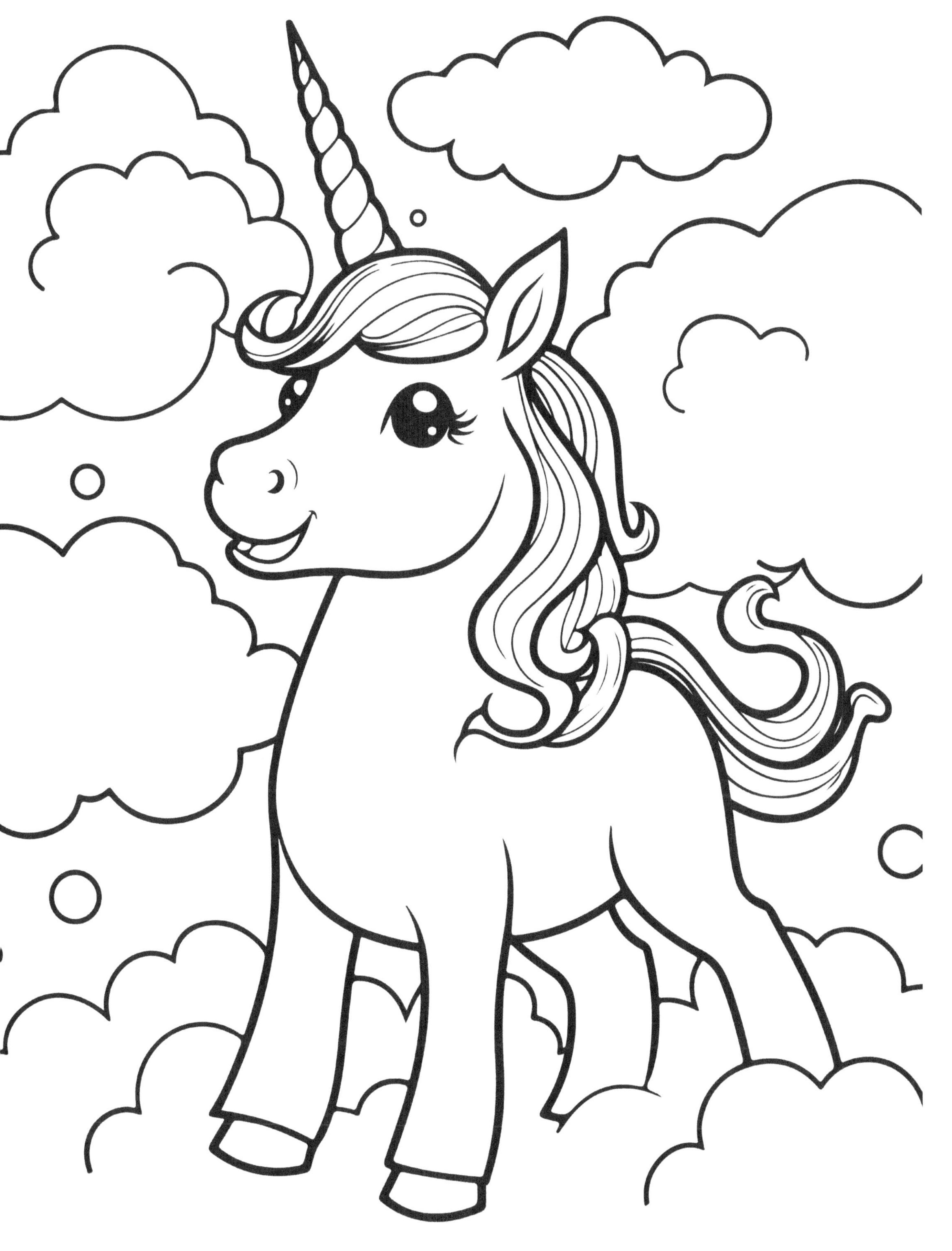

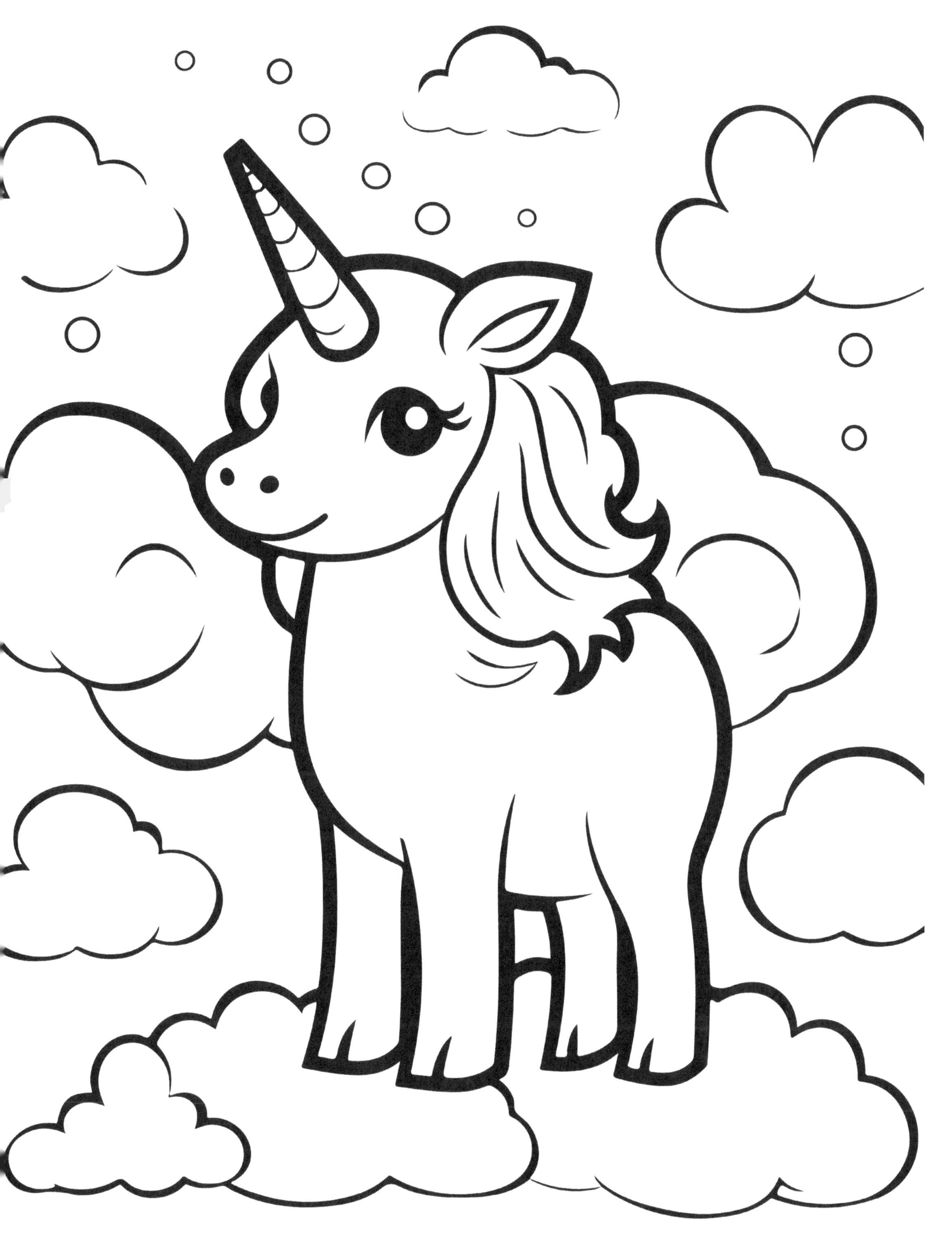

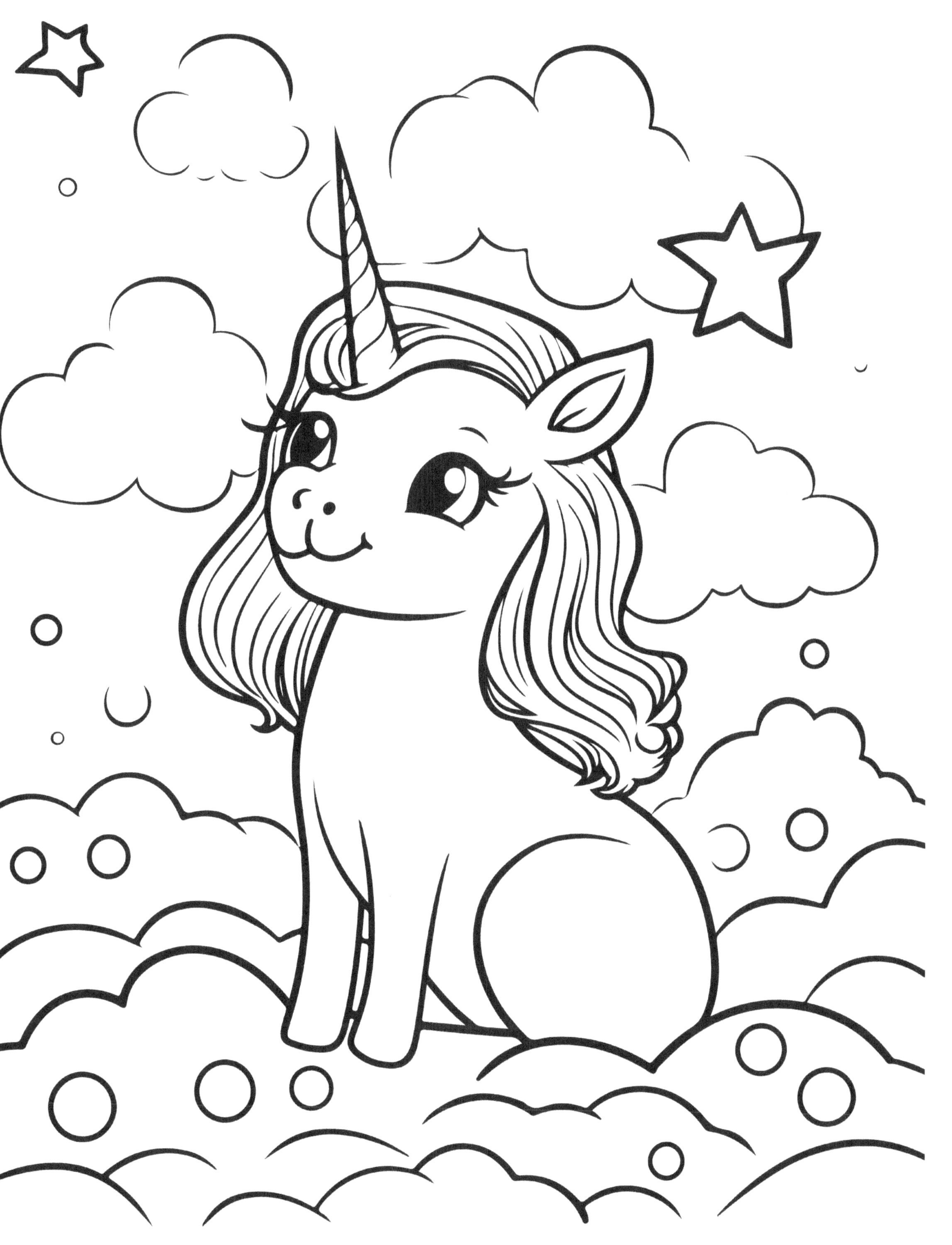

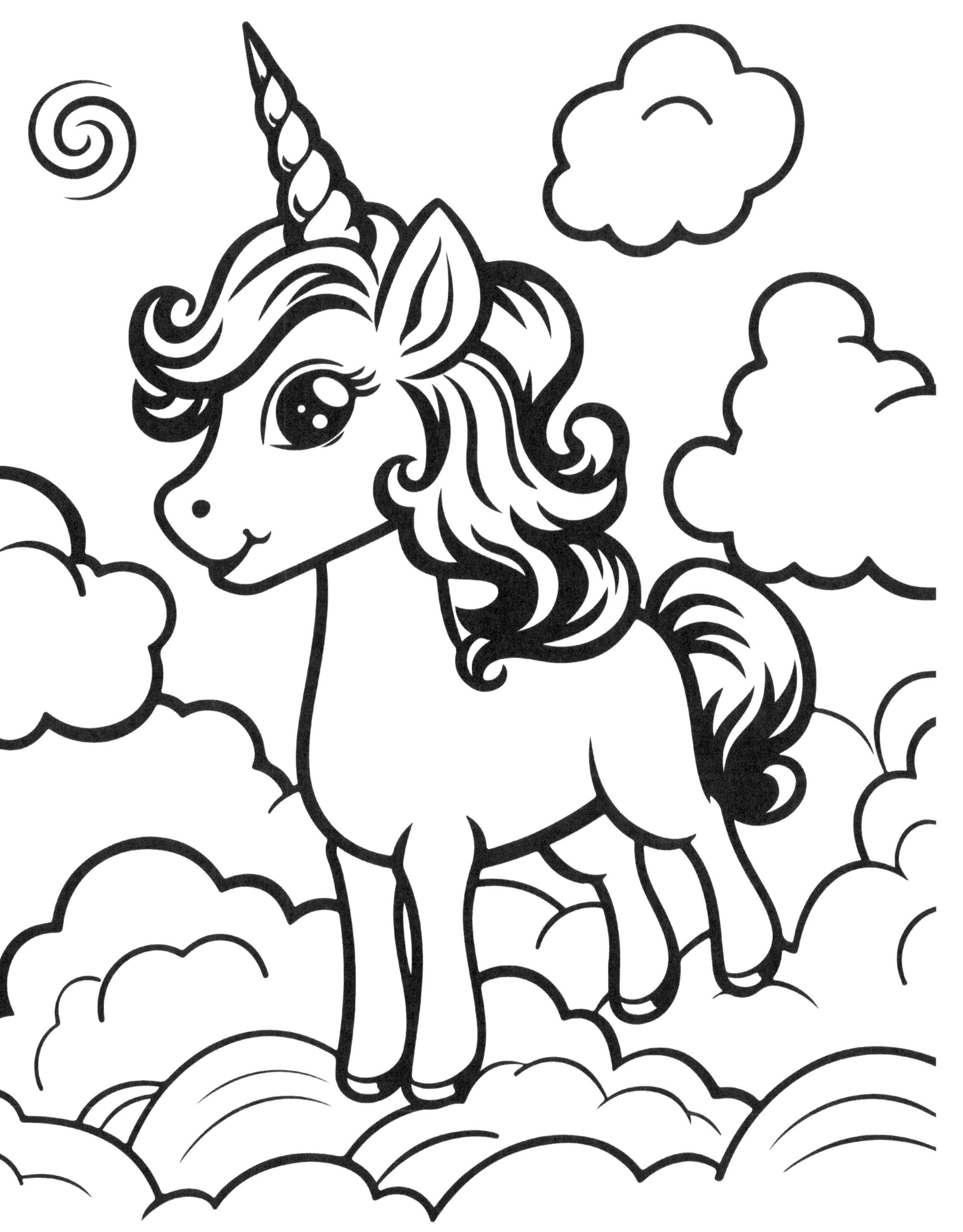

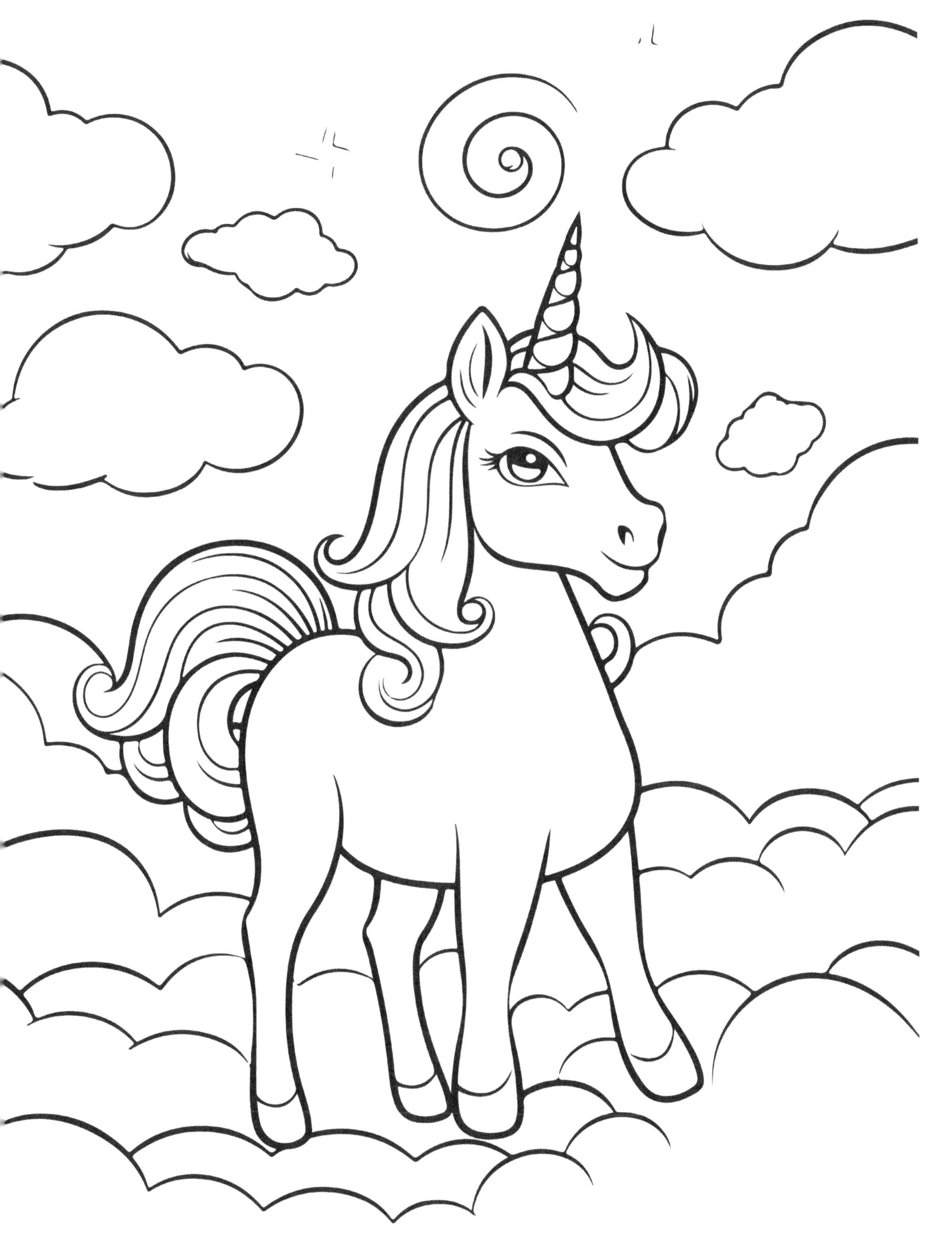

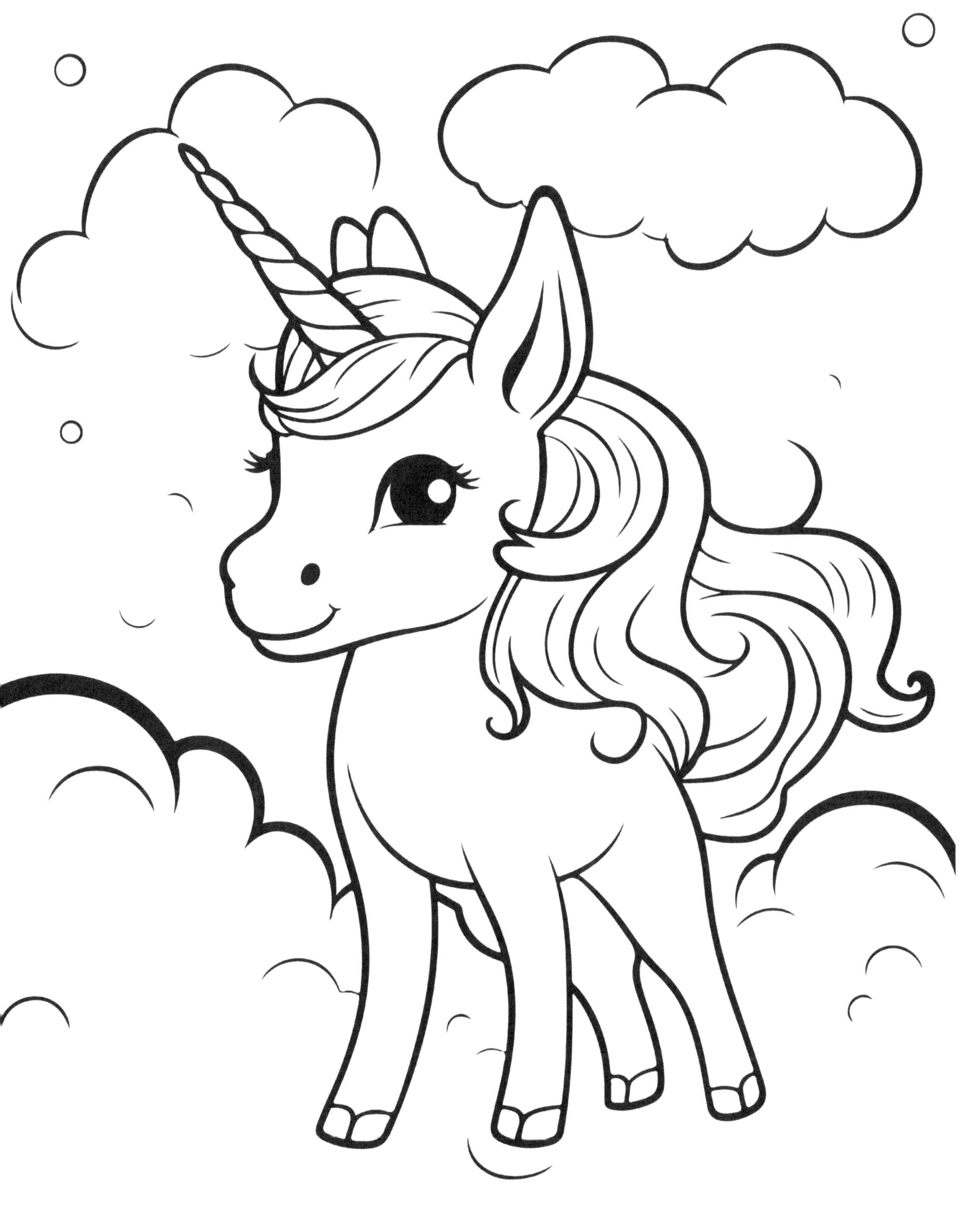

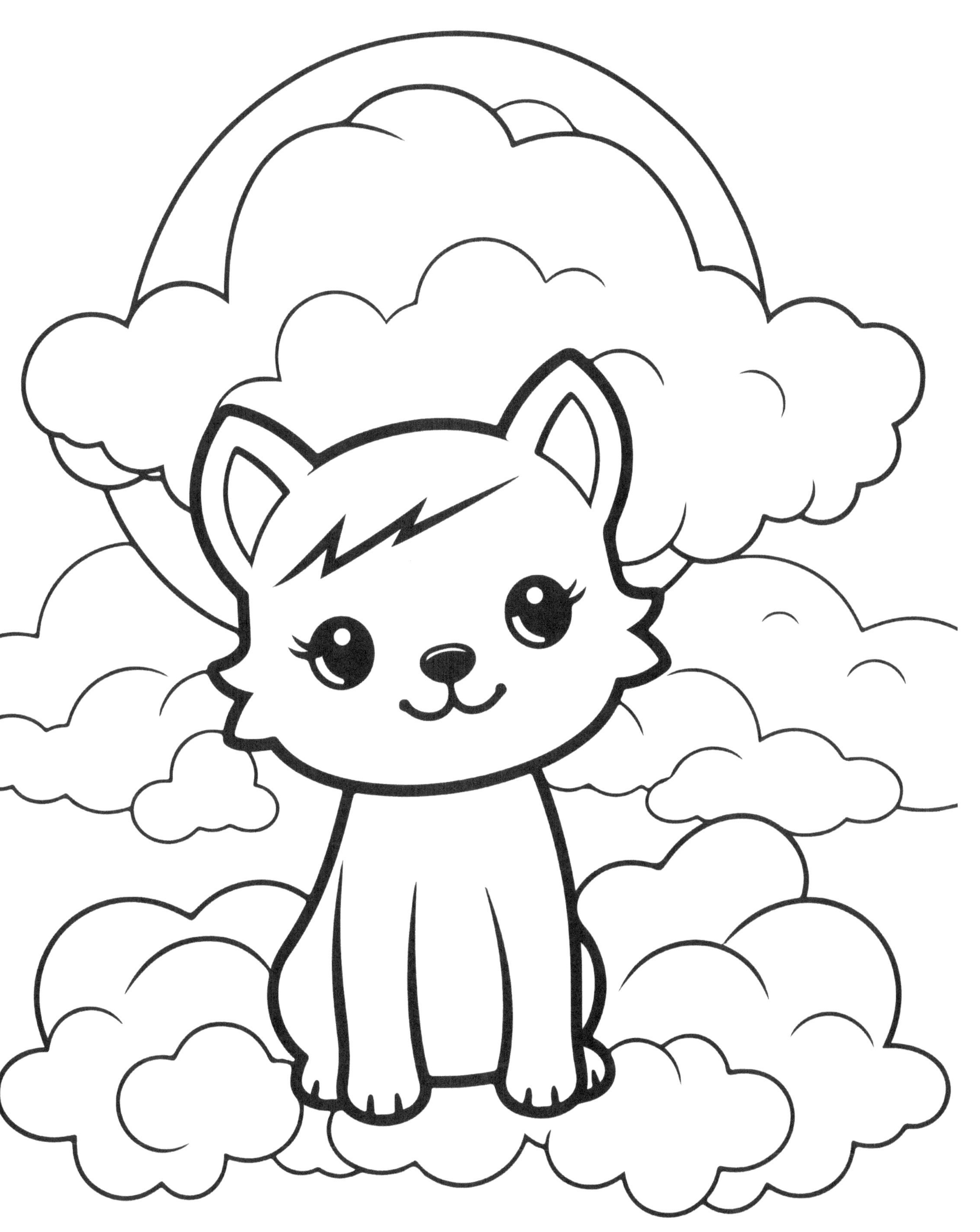

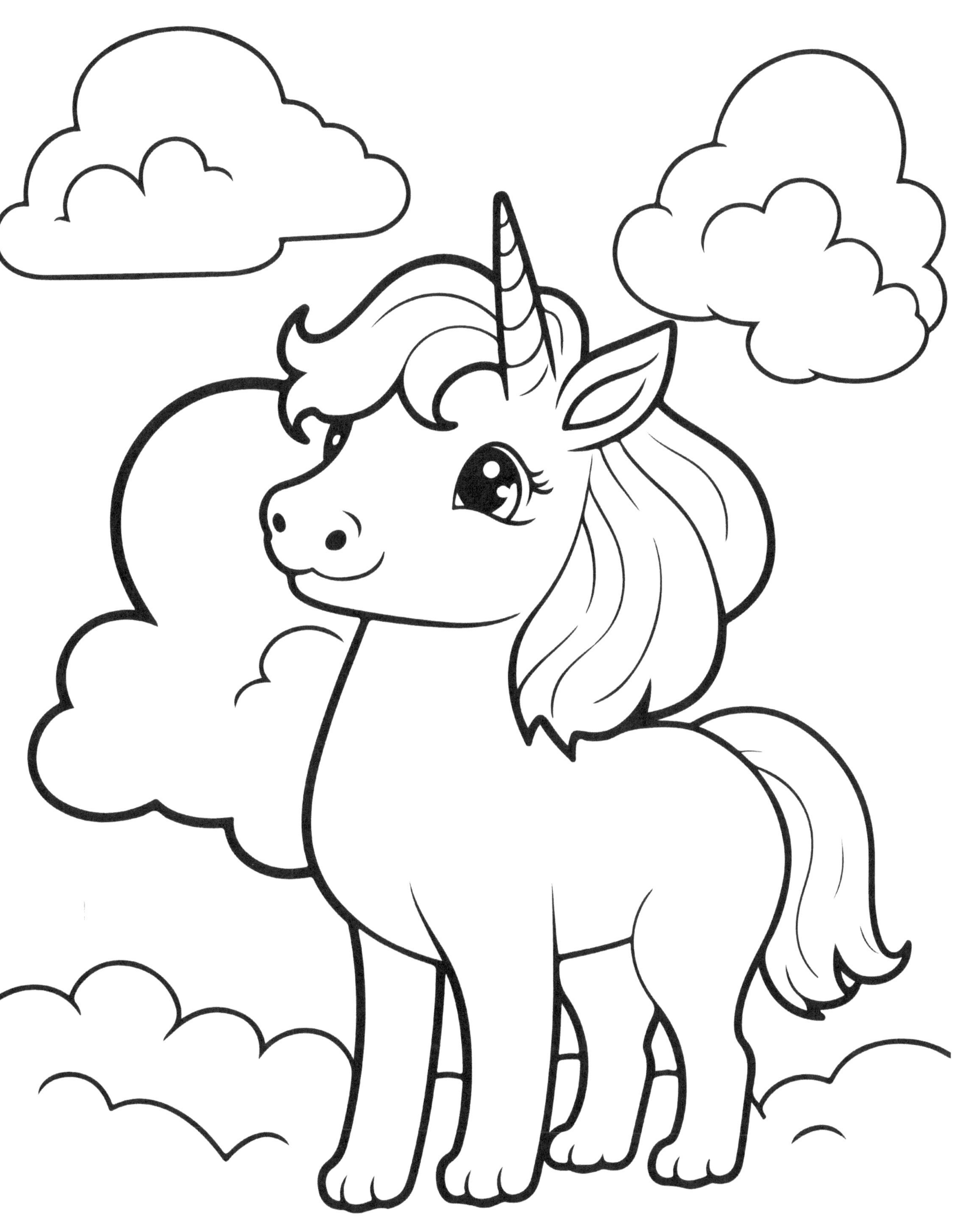